Adam Hart's

e³

e FOR LIFE

3 ELEMENTS FOR ATTAINING ABUNDANT HEALTH & HAPPINESS WITH EASE

FOOD + THOUGHTS + HABITS

Agio
PUBLISHING HOUSE

151 Howe Street, Victoria BC Canada V8V 4K5

*For rights information and bulk orders, please
contact* info@powerofood.com, 1-877-222-2950.

Adam Hart's e3 for Life
ISBN 978-1-897435-45-8 (paperback)

For more information, we invite you to visit
www.PowerofFood.com

Printed on acid-free paper.
Agio Publishing House is a socially responsible company,
measuring success on a triple-bottom-line basis.

10 9 8 7 6 5 4 3 2 1

THANK YOU

Special thanks to my beautiful wife Suzie for all your love
and of course to my mother, who inspires me daily to live my dreams.

I would also like to thank my Toronto, Golden and Squamish family
for nurturing me to a life of abundant health and happiness.
You are all a part of my energy.

Adam Hart

I was once very unhealthy. Despite being pre-diabetic, overweight and suffering from mental illness in the form of depression and anxiety attacks, I was able to regain control over my own health once I discovered the power of food. It was this discovery that allowed me to begin living my life from a place of pure happiness. It was food that was my entry point to attaining a deeper understanding of my ability to heal myself.

I wrote *e3 for LIFE* to share with you the 3 elements for attaining abundant health and happiness with ease – FOOD, THOUGHTS & HABITS. Along the way to regaining control over my own health I stumbled upon a success formula that has the key feature of requiring no restrictions to your diet or lifestyle in any way, with proven results. Yes, I had to make very big sacrifices to discover what I am about to share with you, but you do not have to make any sacrifices to achieve all your desired health goals.

e3 for LIFE takes you on a journey through each of my 3 elements for attaining abundant health and happiness that took me over 10 years to discover. Along the way I will introduce you to a success system within each of the 3 elements that is sure to ease you to better health. It all begins with the FOOD you eat followed by the THOUGHTS you have and concludes with your HABITS that produce your results. Throughout *e3 for LIFE* you will discover tips, secrets, tools and resources that will ensure your ability to take simple action steps for quick and lifelong results.

Through my *Power of Food* events and private coaching clients I have had many requests asking me to share more of my story. I wrote *e3 for LIFE* for you. There is a reason you are here right now and I look forward to being a part of your success.

Adam Hart's

e³

FOR LIFE

3 ELEMENTS FOR ATTAINING
ABUNDANT HEALTH &
HAPPINESS WITH EASE

FOOD + THOUGHTS + HABITS

TABLE OF CONTENTS

FOREWORD

By Dr. Lawrence Klein

As a practicing physician with a passionate 20-year interest in both healing and illness prevention, I consider myself fortunate to know Adam Hart, and to have been exposed – along with many of my patients – to his valuable work over the past several years.

It has finally become clear to most thinking persons (and even the fundamentally conservative modern medical profession!) that diet and lifestyle are the fundamental cornerstones of health – and that without thoughtful attention to these basics, our long-term expectations of a healthy, happy life will be built on shaky ground indeed.

Adam Hart's book *e3 for Life* provides a unique and accessible, non-threatening approach to diet, health, and weight-loss that will prove invaluable for almost anyone, from dietary neophytes to more sophisticated health seekers. The secret, I believe, is in its simplicity and accessibility; as mentioned, *e3 for Life* is non-threatening and non-intimidating, while not in any way sacrificing "content" nor "over-simplifying" important issues. Adam's gift for communicating his passion and excitement for healthy eating (and living!) spill off of every page, to the reader's potentially great benefit!

I've long been fascinated by the profoundly simple yet often-overlooked correlation between diet and health, happiness and longevity. This has led to a fairly voracious perusal of a myriad of diet books, fads and approaches over the years – both personally and vicariously through observing the successes (and unfortunately all-too often the failures) of my patients to lose weight and gain health using these approaches. I (and those patient experimenters in my medical practice) have studied and learned from the likes of: Harvey and Marilyn Diamond (*Fit for Life*), Susan Powter (*Stop the Insanity*), Barry Sears (*The Zone*), Bill Philips (*Body for Life*), Ather Agatston (*The South Beach Diet*), Dean Ornish, and more recently luminaries such as Gabriel Cousens, David Wolfe, and many of their contemporaries in the raw food community. Each of the aforementioned approaches seems to have both proponents and antagonists, and each seems to have its own unique strengths and weaknesses; indeed, at least as compared to the "normal" approach to diet in our society, one could easily argue "most of the available diet books are *mostly* right." In other words, almost any thoughtful approach to eating is somewhat – if not vastly – better than the thoughtless (and often deadly) diet that most North Americans sadly consume; vast quantities of empty calorie foods, frequently as bereft of nutrients as they are laden with toxins! Truly, the accumulated (and ever-growing) mass of convincing studies clearly linking diet, illness, and a bewilderingly large array of diseases should come as no surprise at all.

By the time we reach adulthood, the vast majority of chemicals in our bodies have been replaced countless times; each of our organs and tissues is more-or-less continuously created anew – and always from nutrient building blocks derived from our food. We create ourselves daily with our food and dietary choices, through what we decide to put in our mouths. In a deceptively simple yet truly profound way, our food becomes us – and in the end we truly are what we eat…

Adam's approach to diet and lifestyle reflects an understanding of this truism. The information that he presents is well-considered, nutritionally sound, and nonetheless very accessible to those who don't know what – or how – to eat! And, his recipes are simple and delicious!

So, I'm pleased to welcome you to this wonderful book, which – should you care to embark upon it – has the very real potential to help you to heal your body – and by extension perhaps your life!

Dr. Lawrence Klein

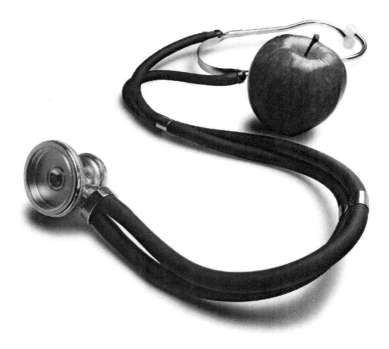

Dr. Lawrence Klein is a well-known and respected physician who has devoted his life to the health of his community.

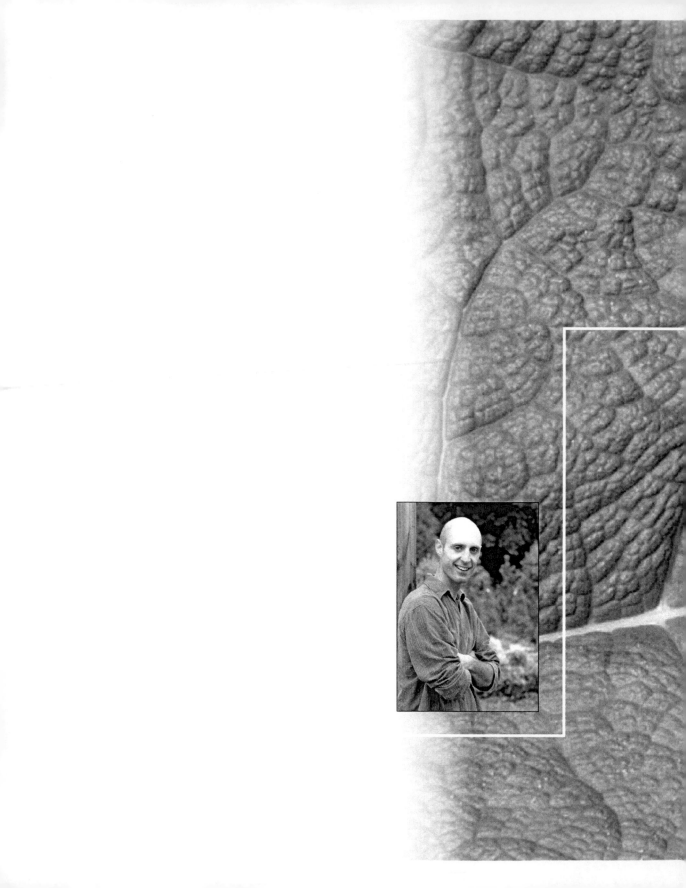

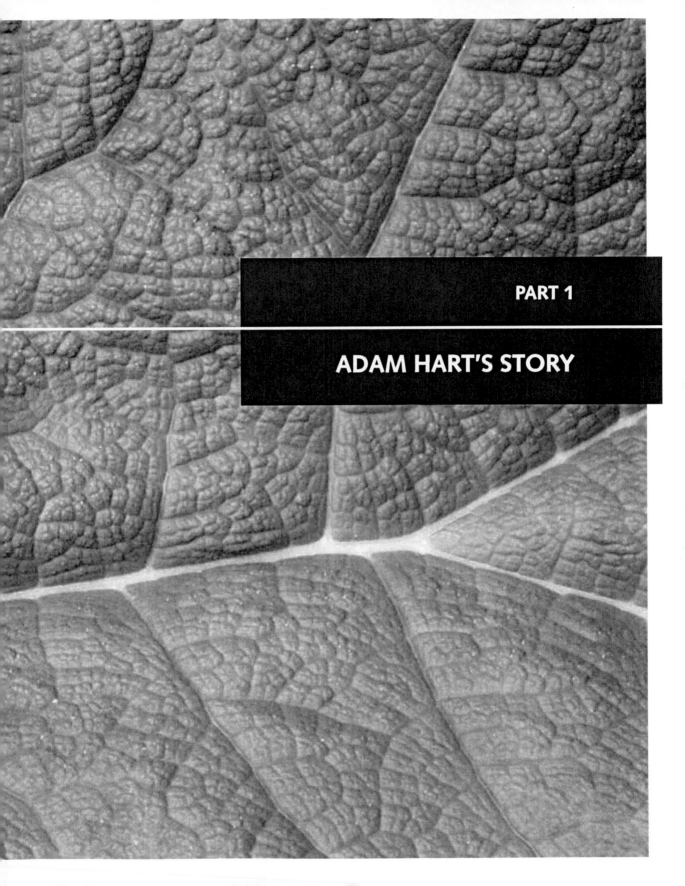

PART 1

ADAM HART'S STORY

DISCOVERING THE HEALTH WITHIN

How many of you suffer from the mid-afternoon crashes or struggle with your weight? How many of you would like to wake up each morning ready to attack your day like a lion full of energy and strength?

These are the same two questions I pose to my audience at each *Power of Food* event. How is it that something as simple as "eating" can cause you so much frustration and stress? Well, the problem lies in finding the right types of food when it comes to healthy eating. We all have to eat to survive. Over the past 50 years many North Americans have taken the enjoyment of food to new heights. When we take a good look at those around us, there is no surprise that we play witness to a lot of overworked, overstressed and overweight friends, family members, neighbors, co-workers and children.

We have become a society disconnected from our relationship with food as well as to our ability to live from a place of purpose and joy. This has left many of us unconsciously struggling to feel alive and healthy. I am here to tell you that it doesn't have to be this way. You have the ability RIGHT NOW to start looking great and feeling even better. I know this first-hand because not too long ago I was part of this unhealthy North American trend. "What?" you are saying to yourselves. "The author of this book was once unhealthy? Naaah, I don't believe it! Adam, tell us your story!"

From a very young age I had a poor relationship with food. It all started with food as a reward.

Take a moment and think about all the different foods you ate when you were young.

Sugar cereals, ice cream, chocolate, cookies, chips, pop/soda are just a few of the most common responses I hear from my audiences. The one big one for me as a child was eating fast food. Yes, I was allowed to go to fast food restaurants as a reward for my good behavior. Like most children of our era, food (especially junk food) was employed by parents as both a reward and a punishment.

These eating habits set me up early on to have a poor relationship with food and helped pave my unhealthy path that led to my dependence on these nutrient-void, harmful foods.

Around the age of 12 or 13 I was diagnosed with ADHD.

ADHD [Attention-Deficit Hyperactivity Disorder] is not a laughing matter. In school, it was commonplace for teachers to pull me out of the classroom, only to be put into a separate room where I could "think" about my behavior. This was both traumatic and humiliating for me. Throughout my teenage years I battled with keeping up in school, always feeling like I had to work harder than all of the other kids just to make the grade. At the age of 13, I was put on Ritalin, a drug that helps one pay attention to tasks, reduce hyperactive behavior, and curb impulsivity. I was drugged to

help control the ADHD. All the while, I had been consuming refined, heavily-processed, convenience foods that provided very little in the way of nutrients and left me starving for strength, energy and brain power. So I ask you, was I suffering from ADHD or from a lack of essential nutrients due to poor food choices?

I now know that a lack of nutrient consumption as a child resulted in my ADHD diagnosis and is a contributing factor in why so many children today are being treated for ADHD. I will admit, mainly with stories from my mother, I was an energetic child who would spend a lot of time bouncing off the walls and causing lots of trouble. I know now the main reason my mother couldn't get me to stop bouncing off the walls had a lot to do with the fact that I lived with a chocolate bar in one hand and a cola in the other.

UNIVERSITY YEARS

My poor relationship with food continued as I put myself through university in Toronto, Canada. During my university days I spent much of my time either shooting pool in the university pub or on the golf course enjoying countless hours searching for the lost balls I would hit. I was not very good. I also spent lots of my time surrounded by the smell of pizza. Why pizza you ask? Well, you see, in order to help pay my way through university I took a job at a pizza restaurant. Growing up, pizza was a main staple in our kitchen, as I know it has and continues to be in many North American households. It just so happens that I became the manager of this pizza restaurant.

Do you have any idea what being the manager of a pizza joint means?

You got it, unlimited access to as much pizza as I could possibly eat. As a young university student with very little cash, I took full advantage of my position. I took such good advantage that by the age of 22 I had reached a weight of 198 pounds, a full 40 pounds heavier than I am today. On a 5'10" frame that's not too bad, but I was overweight and lacking energy.

Eventually I graduated from York University with a degree in Sociology and a postgraduate diploma in International Business Management from Seneca College. I left my pizza job upon graduation

and found myself entering the working world. At 24 years old and still not really knowing myself or what I was capable of becoming, this move into the "rat race" came as a pretty big shock to my system and my health as well.

LIVING UNHEALTHY

With all my time spent playing golf, shooting pool and eating pizza, I look back at my post secondary years in amazement that I was able to graduate all the while having no real clue to my purpose in life. Where was I headed? What was I now going to do with my nicely framed degree and diploma? Confused on what my life's purpose was and where I was supposed to go from here, I decided I would take the easy route and enter into the family business.

Entering the family business was a no-brainer for a kid who really had no idea what to do next. My uncles, who owned an upscale furniture store in Toronto, offered me a position as operations manager.

I settled into my white walled office looking forward to the challenge ahead. I found out very quickly, I was in for a real surprise. My office was a room with no windows, carpet that looked as if it had been salvaged from a demolition site, air circulation comparable to an airplane and a constant computer buzz able to drill a hole directly through the core of my temple. Does that spell out where I had the pleasure of working 8 to 10 hours a day, 6 days a week, with every other week getting a second day off? It's amazing, working for family you would think that things would be a little easier, but as I found out, it was just the opposite.

Within six months of being in charge of up to 30 employees, I had developed what I call extreme stress.

Stress has become an epidemic in our society and, in my opinion, along with our disconnection to our relationship with food, has become the leading cause of the majority of our ailments and diseases. It wasn't too long after my stress levels increased that I started experiencing bouts of depression as well as anxiety attacks. For those of you who have ever experienced depression or anxiety attacks, they are not something to be taken lightly and definitely not fun to endure. In addition to this, I had also been fighting with asthma for many years, and now, all of a sudden I was diagnosed with Fresh Fruit Syndrome. Yes, you heard me right, Fresh Fruit Syndrome ...

... what is that?

That was the question that screamed to me while trying to come to grips with the state of my health. To my surprise my unhealthy state was causing my immune system to crash and my body had started rejecting many of the foods that I had enjoyed eating for years.

Do you have any food allergies or know someone who does?

Out of the blue I became allergic to apples, peaches, pears, plums, carrots, celery and all different kinds of mixed nuts. After doing much research on allergies I came to realize that the more you test food allergies the worse they can get. Boy, did I find that out the hard way having my one and only anaphylactic reaction to eating a hazelnut back in 2000. Allergies are an auto-immune dysfunction. In simple terms, the stronger your immune system becomes, the weaker your allergies will be. I know that fact now because many of my food allergies have been downgraded from anaphylactic to minor intolerances. I credit the strengthening of my immune system over the past several years with my improved health.

Can you relate to stress?

Well there I was, 26 years old living in an overweight body, extremely stressed, experiencing bouts of depression and anxiety attacks, struggling for a decent breath of air thanks to my asthma, and unable to eat many of the foods I love due to Fresh Fruit Syndrome. If all that was not enough,

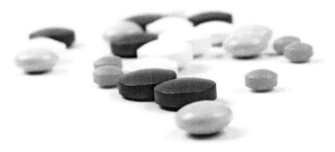

Adam at 26 years old.

I walked into my doctor's office one fateful day in late 2000 and got handed the biggest slap in the face ever. My doctor handed me a prescription for HIGH CHOLESTEROL medication.

Now I have high cholesterol to add to my list?

I stood in front of my doctor with a shocked look on my face and proceeded to ask, "What does high cholesterol mean?"

"*Adam, take this prescription and get it filled. Start on the medication immediately and you will have nothing to worry about.*"

In frustration I blurted out, "But I am already living off several medications – why another one?"

To my surprise my doctor told me, "*Adam, you are essentially pre-diabetic. If you do not begin taking this medication right away you could potentially be insulin dependant within the next six months.*"

Great, so there I was – pre-diabetic.

I had no idea what high cholesterol meant or what being diabetic was all about, and I was stuck with the realization that I would have to live on even more medication. I walked out of my doctor's office totally dejected and frustrated, feeling like a complete failure. My body had been slowly decaying and now my mind had joined in. Welcome to rock bottom Adam and you're only 26 years old. I spiraled deeper into depression for several months while trying to get a grip on my unhealthy state.

MY REBIRTH

Several weeks after having left my doctor's office, I was sitting in a coffee shop, day dreaming, when I clued into something I had never noticed before. I WAS NOT ALONE. I found myself taking a good look around me, there was one gentleman in the far corner with about 4 different pills sitting on the table ready to be popped, a hunched-over elderly woman was sucking on a tank of oxygen, while a friend of mine walked by and said hello who was wearing a medical bracelet which mentioned an allergy to nuts. It dawned on me at that moment that not only was I not alone, but many of my friends, family, co-workers, neighbors and fellow coffee shop patrons were all on similar unhealthy paths. My story was not unique as much as my ego would have liked it to be.

How is it that so many of us have allowed ourselves to become so disconnected to our own health and now rely on medication to feel half human? Not knowing it at the time, I have since discovered that the answers lie within our re-connection to the foods we eat, the shifting of our thoughts from negative into positive and our awakening from the unconscious daily habits we take. Eating unhealthy food, thinking negatively and engaging in limiting habits has conditioned many of us into a life of *humans doing* which is a far cry from living as *human beings*.

HUMANS DOING vs. HUMAN BEINGS

For many years I lived with blinders over my eyes, each day based on basic survival.

Does living as a "Human Doing" relate to you?

My daily priorities consisted of paying my bills, getting my hands on the next hot technological advancement, driving a nice car and watching television on my 42-inch plasma TV, which was a flat screen by the way. All the while I never really was concerned for my health, at least not in a way that could ever really make a difference in a positive direction. At 26 years old, my body and mind had hit a major roadblock. My unhealthy situation was a direct result of living as a "Human Doing" rather than a "Human Being."

Living off medication to help numb the pain of my unconscious, unhealthy life was a conspiracy I had played a role in for quite some time and a conspiracy many of us continue to play everyday. Hitting rock bottom had allowed me to take the blinders off my eyes and play witness to the life I was living. I was now able to take a good hard look at myself and consciously decide to TAKE ACTION and stop relying on all the diets, cleanses, supplements, medication, as well as listening to those around me such as media, doctors, family and friends.

I did not want to be overweight anymore, I did not want to spend another night crying myself to sleep, I did not want to live off prescription drugs to treat my ailments and so on…..

I wanted to start living my life with a healthy body, while living each day from a place of purpose and joy. In order to do so, I knew I needed to say goodbye to the Adam I had known for 26 years and open my heart and mind to the limitless potential I knew existed within ME.

MY 5-YEAR PLAN

Here's a crazy sequence for you, my entire shift in life occurred because I hit rock bottom with my health and then managed to discover abundant energy, decreased stress, controllable asthma, less intense food allergies, lower cholesterol and the reversal of my pre-diabetic state, due to my discovery of – rock climbing!

I'm not suggesting that everyone goes out and starts rock climbing, but indoor rock climbing led to me trying outdoor rock climbing, which led to delusions of grandeur that I could become a mountain guide, which led to my discovery of the Power of Food, which led to me teaching family and friends how to tap into this healing power of food, which led to me creating my own business called the *Power of Food*. How's that for a short timeline version of gaining abundant health and happiness?

It all began with a thought. You see most of my thoughts in the past really never served me in a positive way. Does that sound familiar? Based mostly on anger for being overweight, upset for being depressed, sad for not being able to eat foods I had loved in the past and frustrated for living off medication, my thoughts continuously left me feeling angry, upset, sad, and frustrated over and over again. Once I began to shift my daily thinking to the positive, I was able to create a little clarity providing me with just enough light in my very dark world to ask myself "what would I really like to be doing with my life?" I began creating a 5-year plan to recapture my health and begin taking back control over my life.

The first step was to save up a few dollars to leave work and continue on my journey of self-discovery. I can appreciate the fact that at 26 years old I did not have a mortgage, kids, girlfriend or any other responsibilities that could have held me back from discovering a healthier way of living. I acknowledge everyone who feels they are trapped in their current situation. I am here to tell you that it is never too late to break free and live free, it just requires your unconditional trust and belief that anything and everything is possible. Keep reading and I will tell you how I achieved it.

GET OUTDOORS

Having begun to awaken the health within, thanks to my discovery of indoor rock climbing and eventually outdoor rock climbing, I decided to explore my options in the outdoor adventure world. With money saved up before leaving the "rat race", I planned to give myself one year to break into the outdoor adventure industry. Having enjoyed rock climbing so much I decided to try another outdoor sport: white water canoeing. I signed up for a Swift Water Rescue Course in Ontario and found myself spending that summer working as a canoe guide on rivers in Quebec. What a major life shift in such a short period of time. I enjoyed the summer guiding kids for weeklong trips on rivers such as the Coulonge, Noir and Ottawa. As much as I felt connected to the racing rivers and peaceful call of nature, there was still a pull towards climbing.

During my Swift Water Rescue Course I met a quiet young fellow by the name of Dave. Dave was a small guy, but his ability to maneuver a canoe on the river really left an impression on me. He was a lead guide and instructor at the age of 20. Right away we hit it off. This little skinny kid, who later would become one of my best men at my wedding, gave me the inspiration to leave Toronto to explore the call of the wild in British Columbia, Canada.

If tomorrow you could do anything you'd like, what would it be?

LIFE IN THE MOUNTAINS

Again, my 5-year plan was to spend my first year finding my passion in the outdoors. Having given canoeing a try for one summer season I was now sure my future would have something to do with rock climbing. I had seen movies such as *"Cliffhanger"* and *"Vertical Limits"* which depicted mountain guides jumping off cliffs and clinging to frozen ice or hanging off the edge of a rock like Tom Cruise in the opening scene of *"Mission Impossible"*. The idea of what these movies portrayed was becoming more and more appealing everyday that I spent outside and away from my celled office in

Toronto. I knew these movies were unrealistic portrayals of the mountain life, but the idea of becoming a mountain guide really appealed to me. It was Dave, my canoeing friend, who first mentioned the idea of moving out to British Columbia, Canada. I knew of B.C for some time and for several months prior to working the summer on the rivers I had entertained the idea of moving away from Ontario. Having talked with Dave on several occasions about my desire to explore my options, he quickly offered a very attractive destination.

"Adam, I spend the winters in Golden, B.C., as a ski instructor. Why don't you drive out with me in November and come see what Golden is all about."

That was in September 2001. Two months later I had boxed all my possessions, moved out of my apartment and said goodbye to all my family and friends. Not the easiest thing to do, saying goodbye, but for the sake of my health I knew I had to make the leap out into the unknown.

I did not know this at the time, but this was the Universe handing me a big fat opportunity that I grasped onto as if I were clinging from the mountain top with my finger tips and not willing to let slip away.

November 10, 2001, Dave and I hopped into my VW Jetta and hit the road. We spent the next four days driving across Canada together, settling in Golden some 42 driving hours later and 4500 km away from home. This was to be my first of many winters spent exploring the beautiful mountains of British Columbia, Canada.

"Be open to the opportunities that are in front of you, RIGHT NOW. The Universe is constantly aligning you to receive and experience all your desires."

GLIMPSE INTO THE FUTURE

During my third year of my 5-year plan I moved in with a young quiet guy named Isaac. Isaac was only around 23 when we met. Also from Ontario, he had discovered Whistler as a teenager and then moved to Golden in search of a quieter scene. He was living the life, spending his days skiing big mountains and summers climbing and river rafting. Isaac was smaller in stature, about 5'8", but put him on a set of telemark skis in the mountains and look out. I was truly impressed with his ability to achieve amazing adventures while making it look so easy. Isaac was not the only person I had come to know in Golden who was able to excel in the mountains without much effort. Golden is located within 2 hours of a number of provincial and national parks such as Yoho National Park, Banff National Park, Glacier National Park, Mount Revelstoke National Park and my favorite, Bugaboo Provincial Park. This made Golden the ideal location for aspiring ski, climbing, alpine and all around mountain guides. It didn't take a genius to realize that a pre-diabetic kid from Toronto would have some trouble keeping up in the mountains with such seasoned athletes.

Many of these aspiring guides quickly opened their doors and hearts to this unhealthy specimen so eager to learn and live. My first winter and summer in Golden was spent acclimatizing to my new surroundings and learning how to live and play in the mountains. My second winter and summer in Golden was when I took all the opportunities before me and strengthened my hold on my new life.

Of all my new family in Golden, Isaac was particularly inspirational, although this might be the first time he's heard that. Having spent my first winter and summer discovering cooking and the joy of the stir fry, Isaac had a daily routine when it came to eating that baffled me to no end. You see Isaac was the first guy I had ever met whose cupboard was full of glass jars. Daily, Isaac would open up a few of his jars and begin preparing all kinds of meals. These glass jars were full of different nuts and dried fruits, grains and seeds. This was a strange sight for a kid who grew up on mainly convenience foods. Once I began to incorporate a few of Isaac's strange foods into my diet I experience some profound

Taking the Power of Food *into the Bugaboos for some rock climbing.*

changes to my health as well as in my ability to keep up in the mountains.

DISCOVERING THE POWER OF FOOD

Thanks to the initial inspiration of Isaac's cupboard I spent much of year three of my 5-year plan exploring the mountains and studying food while paying my way through the seasons as a server for a mountain top restaurant. I had spent countless hours studying from hundreds of books all about high cholesterol and what my digestive system was all about.

This initial research led to my discovery of what I now call "The Big Three" – fats, proteins and carbohydrates. These are the essential building blocks to all life and I had taken them for granted my entire life. Understanding how fats, proteins and carbohydrates work for and against my health helped me begin to regain control over my own health without having to spend thousands of dollars relying on diets, cleanses, supplements and prescription drugs.

Wanting to thrive in the mountains, I continued to study how food worked and how my body used food to provide me with proper weight management, abundant energy, increased strength, endurance and all areas of health. I would then spend countless hours in the kitchen creating meals from scratch using all the foods I was learning about such as grains, beans, seeds and nuts as well as fruits and vegetables. Each day was spent learning, creating and playing.

MY DAILY GOLDEN DIET

When I first moved to Golden my daily diet consisted of a very large breakfast bowl of frosted flakes, followed by a peanut butter and jam sandwich for lunch, chocolate bars for snacks and my dinners were mainly stir-frys. By year 3 of my 5-year plan my days started with a fresh bowl of homemade cereal or a smoothie with rice milk, hemp and flax seeds. I would then head out for a day of hard climbing or big mountain skiing with lunch being a packed avocado and almond butter sandwich on sprouted grain bread and homemade power-bars as snacks. My power-bars were made mainly of two ingredients [see recipe section]. Most days would end by creating a new meal based on my most recent research or what I discovered while watching the Food Network during a training session at the gym. I would then proceed to find friends to try my creations. I was so proud of my food that sharing my discoveries and creations became an addiction. Some of the common reactions from friends were:

Dude, where did you learn how to cook like that? Can you show me how to make this? It's awesome, can I have the recipe?

The reactions I received from friends was another big motivator that kept me going into the kitchen and trying new and creative recipes to test in the mountains. Within two years I had transformed myself from severely kitchen illiterate to acquiring life-altering skills in the art of the *Power of Food.* Everything from which foods offered superior nutritional value for optimal health; stocking and storing these key ingredients; how to prepare quick and tasty meals in less time than it takes to eat a fast food happy meal; and how to share this information with friends and family had become my passion and began to provide me with extreme joy.

How many of you have ever experienced pure happiness?

Living each day from a place of pure happiness elevated my inner strength and drove me to strive for something that was beyond my wildest dreams.

PURPOSE IN LIFE

I boarded the plane for a trip back to Toronto in April 2003 with an idea. I was going to introduce my whole family to the *Power of Food.*

Let me back up a bit in time: I had introduced my mother several months earlier to some of the new whole foods I had discovered. We started by introducing her to just a few of the nutrient rich foods that had become a main staple in my diet over the previous year. I showed her how to stock and store these super foods as well as a few easy recipes on how to begin using them daily. Her reaction to the small subtle changes to her diet was a driving force behind eventually turning my passion into a life long goal of sharing the *Power of Food* with others. My mother's excitement when able to manage her weight better, as well as feel an increase in energy thanks to a few subtle small changes, drove her to sharing her discoveries with friends and family. Over the ensuing months, I received a number of emails and phone calls from family and friends all wondering how they too could learn more about the *Power of Food*. I was overwhelmed by the great response and realized that I had stumbled upon something spectacular. The *Power of Food* was something people needed and wanted. Food is the number one contributor to our overall health and was just starting to receive the recognition it deserved. This has a lot to do with our current condition of obesity and diabetes. I had begun to grow into my new

awareness and became empowered by the realization that I had something of value to offer others.

For a period of two months in 2003 while in Toronto, I implemented the first ever *Power of Food Lifestyle Diet Program*. I offered to all my family and friends the opportunity to spend three 1-hour long sessions being introduced to the *Power of Food*. One session would be a walk around their local grocery store revealing all the nutrient-rich foods often found in our local grocery store – but rarely eaten; a second session spent in the kitchen stocking and storing ingredients as well as cooking with these foods; and a third session cooking and talking about personal issues surrounding food. To my amazement the program was a huge success, making an immediate impact on everyone's lives. I knew it would be of value, but the speed in which participants were experiencing profound benefits really solidified for me the healing power of food. Still trying to understand what it was that I had discovered, the feedback I received ensured me that I was on the right track.

At the age of 28 I found my life's purpose. Up until then, I just lived.

Having discovered my purpose in life

– sharing the *Power of Food* – I had only one direction to move and that was to find a way to share this information with as many people as possible. This turned out to be much harder than I could ever have imagined and one heck of a ride that I am still enjoying everyday.

PASSION INTO BUSINESS

Long story short, I moved away from Golden, British Columbia in June of 2004 and made my way to Squamish, B.C., about 45 minutes north of Vancouver where I remain today. This move not only gave me access to some of the best rock climbing in all of North America, but it also provided me with a larger audience. I proceeded to develop my vision of the *Power of Food* and implementing ways to bring my knowledge to the world. This was a lot more difficult than I had expected. I spent the next few years banging my head against the wall doing everything myself from creating my own website to designing my own marketing campaigns and a few catering jobs. Trying to reach the biggest audience I possibly could, I created

programs that would appeal to everyone such as *"Hiding the Health"* which was for families with young kids, *"Wow Your Woman"* which was a men's only cooking class as well as *"Fit Food for Fitness"* which was for athletes trying to reach the next level. I started to stretch myself very thin and began having trouble gaining any ground with any of these programs. Using Squamish as a test ground, I worked diligently to gain attention within the public, but felt like I was swimming up river.

How many of you feel as if you are always struggling trying to swim against the current? I don't recommend trying it, since swimming up river is the quickest way to die from drowning.

Wouldn't your life be so much easier if you could just live each day floating down river without any struggle what so ever?

This is the idea of living from a place of pure happiness. When you discover this place, everything in life seems to just flow with ease. I had glimpses of what this felt like, but was not yet floating downstream with the current, with ease.

Having spent years four and five of my five-year plan reinventing the *Power of Food* to reach a larger audience, somewhere around the end of my grand plan, during year five, I stumbled upon the realm of corporate wellness. The idea of so many North Americans sitting behind a desk eating foods that lead to the mid-afternoon crashes and struggling with weight held a soft spot in my heart because that was me only six years earlier. I decided to put together a one-hour presentation on the importance of healthy eating in the workplace for overall health as well as for the health of the organization. To my surprise the first place I introduced the presentation was looking for a workplace wellness program on increasing energy. I was so excited to have finally found a place where there was a solid demand for my message.

Over the next several months I continued to produce wellness options for corporations based on the *Power of Food,* all the while growing into my new brand and marketing push focused on strengthening *Adam Hart's Power of Food* position in the corporate wellness market. I had begun to own my own power to a new degree, without my ego getting in the way. I have always come from a place of integrity, no ulterior motives, no unrealistic diets or artificial supplements to sell, just pure truth.

I was not putting myself out there looking for what others could provide me for my time, but rather what could I provide others with the time they provided me. Knowing that I could truly make a healthy difference in others' everyday actions allowed me to share my personal story with hundreds of people and soon thousands. Over the next two years I firmly established my position in the corporate wellness world and was finally able to see my years of effort to bring the *Power of Food* to a larger audience become a reality. Seeing my creation begin to affect the lives of thousands of others brought me pure happiness. It was this happiness that led me to seeking a larger audience and is the reason you are reading this book right now. It was you who asked for this book and it is my coming-out party as I continue to spread the *Power of Food* around the globe.

Welcome to the *Power of Food* movement!

Adam Hart's **Power** of **Food**

WHY  FOR LIFE

2ND GENERATION FAST FOOD EATER

I don't remember the date, but some time after my move to British Columbia I was back for another visit to Toronto. It was during a visit with my grandparents when I discovered something profound. While searching my grandmother's cupboards looking for her family famous cookies, I noticed something about her shelves. All her shelves were full of glass jars. To my surprise, the jars were filled with nuts, seeds, grains, beans and dried fruits just like the way my own kitchen was now set up. It dawned on me that this was a lost style of eating that for generations kept humans strong and healthy. Somewhere over the past 60 years many of us gradually lost our connection to the importance of food and how powerful nutrition is for maintaining optimal health. Our over-dependency and obsession with fast and convenient foods has led many North Americans into a state of obesity and diabetes as well as being

over-stressed and unhappy. I call this the "2nd Generation Fast Food Eater" disease.

I am a second generation processed and fast food eater. Think about that for a moment: we are at a situation in history that has never been experienced before, both in the quality of food we eat and in our unhealthy condition. One of the most popular fast food restaurants first opened its doors in the early 1950s out of California and at the same time we were introduced to the first home frozen meals. Frozen TV dinners gained popularity very quickly as did the fast food craze, to the point where many households in North America began experiencing a shift in their relationship to food. It should be no surprise that when you Google statistics on obesity or diabetes, you discover there is a direct correlation between the growth of obesity and diabetes through the generations in relations to the rise in the availability of processed foods in North America. Within a relatively short period of time, heavily-refined, processed foods had become conveniently available across North America to help immediately curb hunger cravings. They are cheap, they taste salty, fatty and sugary, they please the eye and they are available everywhere. The convenience of processed food and our lack of awareness to the damaging effects of these foods is a major reason for the decline in the health of North Americans over the past 60 years.

The *Baby Boomer* generation, who are now in their 50s and 60s, were for the most part the first generation to feed their children fast, over-processed food. Before the *Baby Boomer* generation, processed food did not exist to the extent that they exploded in the late 1960s, '70s and '80s. By the early '80s and into the '90s the processed food craze had grown into a major convenient solution for many *Baby Boomers* as they struggled with juggling multiple children and duel income situations. Following the *Baby Boomer* generation was *Generation X. Generation X*, now in their 30s and 40s, started feeding their kids processed foods right from a young age. Many *Generation Xers*, like myself, grew up on processed food and were never educated on healthy eating whether in school or at

home. During the same time there was a sharp rise in big box grocery stores, which led to a further disconnect from local and unprocessed foods. Both the *Baby Boomers* and *Generation Xers* were choosing to eat and choosing to feed their loved ones nutrient-deficient food.

As North Americans, over the generations, continued to embrace processed foods and all their perceived benefits, we played witness to the rise of a third generation of processed food eaters, *Generation Y*. *Generation Y* were next in line to inherit our love/addiction for processed food. This generation not only consumed processed foods at alarming rates, but they began feeding their kids, the so-called *Millennia Generation* the same unhealthy foods void of vital nutrients, leading to *another* sharp rise in obesity and diabetes amongst adults and children In North America.

Now we get to present day where we find so many of our friends, family members, co-workers, children and so on struggling to feel well and challenged to maintain a level of energy to get them through each day. Whether it is cancer, heart disease, diabetes or obesity, many of our current health conditions have their roots in our relationship with food. Why should it be surprising to see so many North American adults and children relying on diets, supplements, cleanses, vitamins and pharmaceuticals to help alleviate their individual ailments – I know I did. I spent thousands of dollars on protein shakes and prescription drugs, the newest fad diet and the latest brand of vitamin all to help treat my many ailments. Many of these options only led to me feeling worse. Every diet I had ever been on ended in failure and only led to more feelings of guilt, frustration and anger. On top of that I always gained more weight at the conclusion of each diet.

Does this description apply to you or someone you know?

Like many others looking to feel healthy, I did not know what to do or where to begin. Nothing was setting me up to lose weight, feel more energy and get off my prescription drugs. Essentially my body was in constant dis-ease. My daily medication only masked my underlying health problems. I didn't know what to do to feel better. I was constantly frustrated, angry and unhappy. My body was lacking vital nutrients due to my processed food diet, and my mind was suffering because of

my unhappy thoughts that led to feelings of frustration, anger and guilt about my unhealthy state. Combined together, poor food and damaging thoughts meant I was locked in depression for several years.

Our fast paced lives and disconnect with food has led the *Baby Boomers, Generation Xers, Generation Y* kids and now the *Millennias* (the children of Generation Y) into a state of confusion around how to prevent or cure dis-ease in our bodies and minds. One thing we have become very good at is our grasping for the next one-of-a-kind quick fix solution, of which the majority only mask our conditions and do nothing to reconnect us to our own vitality.

Regaining control over your own health does not have to be complicated or a daunting task. The answers to gaining abundant health and happiness begin within reconnecting to your relationship to *food* and beginning to engage your *thoughts* and

habits in a new light. It is these three fundamental elements that are at the heart of *e3 of LIFE*.

NOT ANOTHER DIET!

First I would like to mention my displeasure with the word *diet*. So many of my past clients have mentioned to me in confidence how the word diet conjures up very heavy emotions. I want to acknowledge the trauma that this word may hold for you as it once did for me.

Why is it that we have been subjected to countless diets since the mid 1950s? What makes us all so different that we need to have multiple diets all with promises of releasing us from our feelings of guilt, anger and frustration through the improvement of our weight or diabetic states?

Now I don't want to get too political here, but diets are a very big business – a multi-billion dollar a year industry. It's supply and demand at its most basic form. The demand is at an all time high and is only getting higher as the rise in obesity and diabetes reaches epidemic proportions. With the rise in demand we see a rise in supply. If you take a look at the history of diets you can see that as obesity has grown through the years so has the supply of diets available. It is this basic law of supply and demand that has driven the diet industry for decades. Bombarded by countless claims of being our next salvation, choosing to diet is like choosing one of the 31 flavors of your favorite ice cream. The diet you choose may help you feel better about yourself for a little while, but in the end most diets only lead to failure.

The problem lies within the concept of diets. Defined as a regulated selection of food, diets do not set you up for long term success. This is because diets are a one-dimensional solution. As a one-dimensional solution, diets do nothing to get to the roots of why you do what you do, why you take the daily actions you take and only leave you back at square one with a lighter wallet and feelings of frustration and guilt. Like prescription drugs and synthetic supplements, most of which I also classify as a one-dimensional solution, diets do nothing to set you up for long term success and only restrict you from something, causing conflict. In order for you to experience abundant health you must look at the roots

of why you are unhealthy. How did you get to this point in your life feeling the way you feel, having the results you have? The reality is, it all comes down to three fundamental elements – *FOOD, THOUGHTS* and *HABITS*. As I discovered many years ago, if you want to stop spending all your time, energy and money on one dimensional solutions, you must engage these three elements to attain abundant health and happiness.

THE 3 ELEMENTS

The 3 elements for abundant health and happiness are the FOOD you eat, the THOUGHTS you have and your HABITS.

FOOD

Food is the first element for attaining abundant health and happiness with ease. Have you ever been on a diet before or altered your diet to try to get a little healthier? I know I have and each time I tried a diet or meal plan it only left me feeling more confused about food and what I needed to do to be healthier. With so much confusion around healthy food along with our disconnection with our relationship to food, it is almost impossible for us to use food to gain better health, unless we understand the basics behind food. I am not saying that you can't be successful dieting, but the majority of us are preconditioned to fail. It is in this failure that we continue to sabotage our ability to regroup and really get a handle over our diabetic or obese state.

"Let food be your medicine and medicine be your food." ~ Hippocrates

In order for us to regain control over our own health we must reconnect to the foods we eat and learn how to make eating healthy easy. *e3 for LIFE* will introduce you to the number one secret the food industry does not want you to find out. I will also teach you how to increase the nutritional value of the foods you already love to eat without any drastic changes to your diet and lifestyle. With no restrictions to your diet, the systems revealed in the *FOOD* section of *e3 for LIFE* will set you up for long-term success that you can be proud of. Food is the cornerstone of your health and I will show you how easy it can be for you to begin losing weight, attaining abundant energy and relieving unwanted stress.

THOUGHTS

Thoughts are the second element for attaining abundant health and happiness with ease. Your success for achieving abundant health begins with what you put into your mouth. It makes perfect sense that everything you eat needs to feed your body with vital nutrients to stay alive, but what about your mind? Yes, food plays a big role in the health of your mind, but your thoughts have more power over your results than anything else you do and they impact your health in more ways then you could ever imagine. In this section I will reveal the simple system I designed for engaging my thoughts and ensuring they bring positive results.

With the minds of so many of us being dominated by negative thoughts, it is no wonder so many of us look for a quick fix from solutions that don't provide long term success. When you finish reading this section you will have no more excuses for self sabotage. You will have the ability to control your thoughts and wield their power to make all your dreams reality.

HABITS

Habits are the third element for attaining abundant health and happiness with ease. Becoming aware of your limiting, junk habits is at the core of getting to the roots of why you do what you do, and having the ability to shift their impact on your health. We all have damaging habits that impact our health. You may overeat, or eat out of emotions; maybe you get angry while driving and scream at the top of your lungs on occasion. How about smoking or not exercising? These are all limiting habits that damage your ability to be healthy. When you acknowledge your habits you can begin to trace them back to where they come from. Where do your limiting, junk habits come from? Read this chapter and discover how you can take back control and turn your junk habits into a positive success you can celebrate and be proud of.

When you complete the pages of *e3 for LIFE* you will have all the tools, secrets, and resources necessary to begin feeling abundant health and happiness with ease. No more excuses, no more self doubt, no more feelings of guilt and frustration, just pure happiness knowing that you now have the power to engage your health in a positive way and build a strong foundation for long term sustainable results. *FOOD, THOUGHTS* and *HABITS* are the cornerstone of your existence and by engaging all three at the same time you will be setting yourself up with a lifestyle system for attaining unimaginable dreams and vibrant health. This is what *e3 for LIFE* makes easy for you to achieve. Do you want it? If you are ready, then begin now!

IT'S TIME TO BEGIN *e3 for LIFE.*

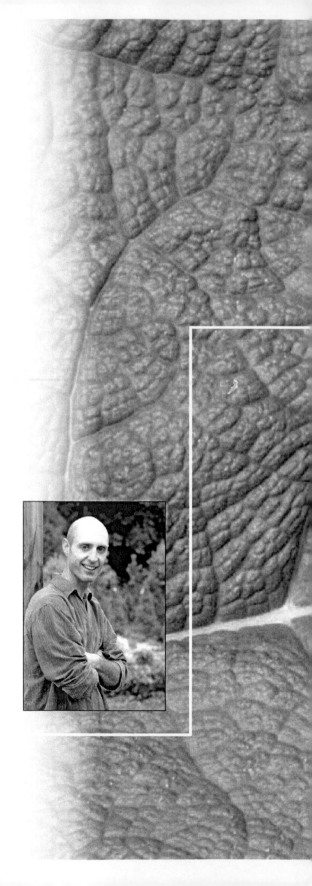

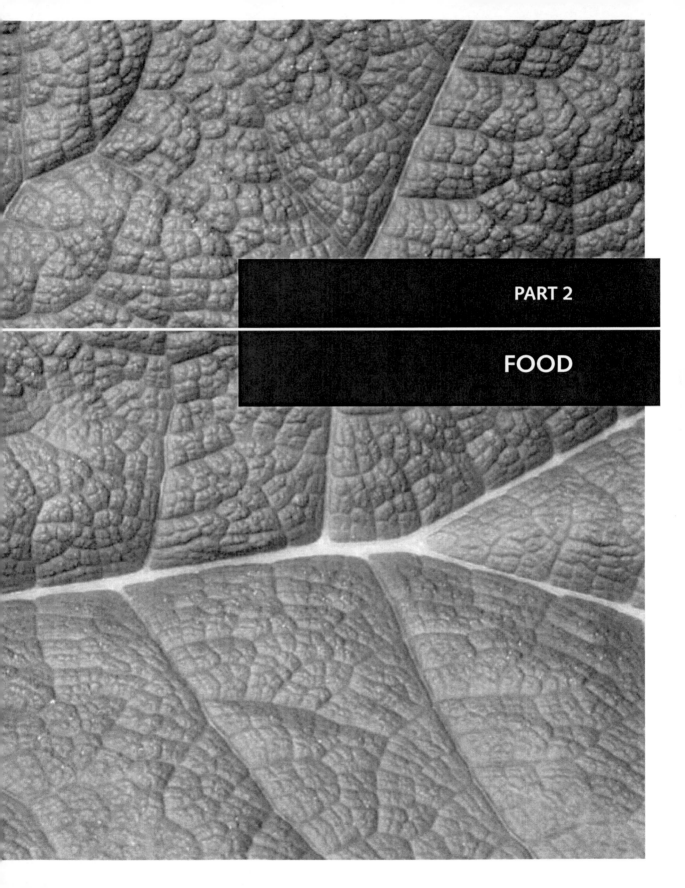

PART 2

FOOD

WHY THE BIG SECRET

Once I started cooking for myself everything changed. Having grown up on primarily processed, refined foods, I never realized how much my body and mind were starving for health. Once I got into the kitchen and began to explore food in a new way, I quickly unlocked one of the key elements to gaining back control over my own health.

What was it that I had discovered about food and why was it a secret until now?

Did you know that there are over 300,000 thousand choices of food to select from in North America? Even more alarming is the fact that depending on which grocery store you visit, you may find up to 30,000 to 60,000 choices. That's a lot of choice.

Do you find it confusing walking through your local grocery store?

Eating healthy does not have to be confusing!

The desire to eat healthy has gained momentum over the past decade due to the rise in obesity, diabetes, heart disease, cancer and many other illnesses. With so much confusion surrounding the foods we eat and whether they are healthy or not, many of our friends, family members, neighbors, co-workers and children resort to one-dimensional solutions such as diets, supplements, cleanses and prescription drugs just to get some relief. There has never been a better time to get back to basics when it comes to the food you eat.

What if I told you that in the past I had to make very drastic changes to my diet and lifestyle to regain control over my own health, but you do not have to in order to begin feeling healthy again – would you want to know how to do it? Having the ability to get healthy without any diet restrictions or lifestyle changes are at the core of why *e3 for LIFE* is so successful and why you will experience success as well.

What happens if you restrict yourself from something?

More often then not, you will want that food even more then before – because you are focusing so much attention on it. What is at the heart of most diets? They restrict you from something! This is the major reason why diets don't work and why the system I am about to introduce to you will set you up for a lifestyle and will allow you to maintain your health goals long term. It all begins with becoming a little more familiar with what food is all about.

Food selection does not have to be so complicated. The reality is, it all comes down to one big, hidden secret about food. Are you ready for the big answer, the universal law of food, the key to unlocking your ability to heal with ease? Okay, okay, here it is, it all comes down to this:

The Big Secret is…… there are only two kinds of food – that's it.

There is the answer to the big mystery, the key to cutting out any more confusion you may have about food. There are only two types of food. Do you want to know what they are?

- **Whole, Plant-Based Food**
- **Processed Food (includes meat)**

You are either eating a whole, plant-based food or you are eating processed food.

WHOLE FOOD REVOLUTION

After spending countless hours dissecting through all the information available on the healing power of food I came to realize that in the end, no matter what you read in the newspaper or on-line, no matter what your co-workers are talking about at the office, your ability to get healthier all comes down to eating more whole, plant-based foods.

Let me guess: you are wondering, *"what are whole foods?"*

I asked myself the same question many years ago. I define whole foods as *foods that have not been broken down, altered or transformed in any way*. Whole foods are in their complete state and offer superior nutritional value when compared to processed foods, which are mostly void of vital nutrients or excessive in their forms such as many meat options. There are only

6 whole, plant-based foods and, when included as a part of your daily diet, they have the ability to heal the disease within both your body and mind. The 6 whole foods are foods that come from the soil beneath your feet and the living plants that surround you. In no particular order they are:

NUTS & SEEDS
GRAINS & LEGUMES
FRUITS & VEGETABLES

Yes, these may all sound familiar to you and they may even be a large part of your diet already. I told you this was not going to be complicated. Many of these foods you already have in your kitchens. The problem lies in the fact that in North America the majority of our diets relies on a heavy dose of meat consumption or foods that used to be a whole food and by the time you consume them, they have been so heavily processed that they are depleted of most of their nutritional qualities.

Here are a few examples of processed foods that most North Americans consume on a daily basis:

- Bread, pasta, cookies, muffins, crackers, soda, fast food, and

- Meat (which I define as chicken, eggs, pork, lamb, red meat, fish, turkey and dairy).

I am not suggesting that you eliminate these foods from your diet. What I am suggesting is that by getting closer to the true source of your food in the form of whole plant-based foods, you will begin to provide your body with vital nutrients it is starving for right now.

When talking about whole foods I am talking about a style of eating that is a lifestyle diet. A lifestyle diet is very different from conventional diets of which the majority only set you up for failure. *e3 for LIFE* makes it easy for you to introduce whole foods into your daily diet without restricting you from eating the foods you already love to eat. It's all about bringing in a source of light – and not about removing the darkness, which is often a losing battle.

PAINTING THE PICTURE

Now that you have a better understanding what whole foods are, I want to paint you a picture. This picture is to help shed some light as to the difference between whole foods and processed, refined foods. Let me ask you a question;

In North America, what is our main grain?

If you said *wheat* you would be correct. In Asia the main grain is rice and depending on where you go throughout the world it may be something different, but in North America it's wheat. Now let's take a quick look at a typical North American farmer. A wheat farmer has his fields of wheat. The wheat is in its whole state. It has not been broken down, altered or transformed in any way and contains its full nutritional value, lots of protein and complex carbohydrates. In order to make a living the farmer must harvest the wheat and ship it out for production. Once harvested, the wheat grain is sent to the milling process. During the milling process the wheat is ground finely and broken down, mainly using a heat process, which kills the majority of the nutritional value. In modern agriculture, using heat is the most efficient way to process a grain into flour, and the quicker the production the bigger the dollar.

Once you mill the wheat, you have flour. There are a few processes that are less harmful when processing grains such as stone grinding or steel cut, but the majority of our commercial wheat flour in North America uses a heavy heat process that kills most of the nutritional value. This heat-processed flour is the main ingredient in the majority of our commercial food products, such as breads, crackers, cereals, cookies and pasta.

With very little to offer in the way of nutritional value, our-over consumption of these typical foods only provide us with empty calories. The empty calories we receive from processed foods leave our bodies and minds starving for energy while fattening our waistlines.

Can you relate to mid-afternoon crashes? How about food cravings?

I used to be known around my office as the chocolate guy. My office drawer was like a vending machine full of chocolate bars. Each bite helped boost me with a burst of quick energy, but always left me with a big energy crash and heading back to my desk drawer for another hit.

Can you relate to being the chocolate guy or girl in your office?

If you are struggling to stay awake throughout your day, if you are wondering how you can lose those dreaded last ten pounds you have wanted to get rid of for years, if you struggle with diabetes or heart disease, it is time to start looking at the foods you are eating.

Most of our eating choices rely on processed foods that are quick, easy, taste good, cheap and can conveniently be found at almost any gas station, corner shop or grocery store. Processed foods do not provide you with key nutrients and only feed you simple carbohydrates in the form of sugar or other ingredients that quickly turn into sugar. Because most of our diets are made up of simple foods void of vital nutrients, this means we are in a constant battle to keep a steady stream of energy flowing throughout our days. With so much confusion around food and our inability to use foods to support our health, we continue to grab the convenient, tasty and cheap option that keep us in a addictive, vicious cycle of struggling to get a handle on our health. If you want to stop struggling and start thriving, a basic knowledge of what the three key nutrients are and what foods offer the ideal amounts is your starting point.

Food is made up of what I call *The Big Three*. *The Big Three* are the essential building block to all life. Without them you would not be alive today. *The Big three* are FATS, PROTEINS and CARBOHYDRATES. A basic understanding of *The Big Three* is vital for you to be able to really become aware of how harmful of a diet you may currently be eating and the simple steps you can take to begin to see a shift in your health.

THE BIG THREE

There is so much confusion around food that you may not even be familiar with the importance of *The Big Three* or the ideal foods in order to make sure you consume a healthy amount of them. One of the underlying harmful effects that dieting has on your health is the fact that many diets *restrict* you from one or all of *The Big Three*. For example, one of the most popular diets for that past 20 years restricts your intake of carbohydrates while another more recent fad diet tries to get you to eliminate all fat from your diet. Both of these approaches can be quite damaging to your health and do nothing to set you up with long term, healthy eating habits.

So what is the problem with restrictions? We already discussed earlier that any restrictions leads to pain and eventually a desire for more of what we can't have. What lies even deeper is the harmful affect you may be experiencing from restricting yourself of one of *The Big Three* and missing out on the important role it plays in keeping you healthy.

Fats, proteins and carbohydrates are vital for optimal health and play key roles in disease prevention. If you restrict yourself from one of these key nutrients as often found in popular diets, you are causing your body more harm than good. The difference in being healthy or being sick lies in your ability to distinguish between the quality of fats, proteins and carbohydrates you consume. I promise that if you think of your food in quality terms when it comes to *The Big Three*, you will gain the power to choose healthier essential fatty acids, quality complex carbohydrates and easily digestible complete protein sources with ease. Now let's give you the power to make the healthy choice the easy choice. Let's begin with fat.

FAT

Fat in North America has a very negative connotation to it. You hear the word fat used in specific media news stories, advertisements, and product sales or in your daily conversation at the office or home. Very rarely will you hear fat being used in a positive way. So why have we become a society terrified of fat? It is very hard to think of fat in healthy terms, but that is just what you have to do. Throw out every negative idea you have around fat and embrace it for the abundant and vital function it serves in your ability to feel and look healthy. Fat is both good and bad when it comes to consumption. For decades saturated fats have been vilified in North American and more recently trans fats have received the same recognition. The truth is a large part of the processed food market is comprised of some form of saturated fat or trans fat. Why is this a bad thing? Some saturated fat is actually healthy for you such as the saturated fat found in coconut oil, but for the purpose of our discussion, we will look at saturated fats and trans fats as the types of fats you want to avoid.

SATURATED FAT

So what is so bad about saturated fat? Saturated fat is fat that is solid at room temperature. It is more stable and less chemically active than unsaturated fats and therefore tends to stick together in your body. Do you remember the last time you cooked a pan of bacon? What happened to the grease 10 minutes after you were done? It congeals into a white semi-solid form, a perfect example of saturated fat. That is what happens inside your arteries when you consume excessive amounts of saturated fat; this increases your risk of developing heart disease, stroke and diabetes. Saturated fats are found mostly in firm fats that come from animal food sources such as red meat, butter, milk, yogurt and cheese.

TRANS FATS

Trans fats are created in an industrial process that adds hydrogen to liquid vegetable oils to make them more solid. Another name for trans fats is "partially hydrogenated oils." The process of hydrogenation adds hydrogen atoms to unsaturated fats, making them into partially or completely saturated fats. This means that trans fats are the equivalent of saturated fat, but they are man-made through the hydrogenation process. There are a few naturally occurring trans fats, but the majority is produced through an industrial process.

Modern food manufactures prefer using trans fats because they have a higher melting point then other fats, which makes them more attractive for baking. It is also very popular because the saturation in trans fats extends their shelf life. Did you know that most grocery stores will not carry food on their shelves unless it will last at least six months. This makes trans fats very appealing. They are also popular for food manufacturers because trans fats are inexpensive to produce and give foods a desirable taste and texture. Many restaurants and fast-food chains use trans fats to deep-fry their food because oils with trans fats can be used many times in commercial fryers. This is a huge money saver even though it is very damaging to your health.

Trans fats can be found in many foods. The most popular foods where trans fats can be found are fried foods like french fries, doughnuts, cookies, crackers, pie crusts, pastries, pizza dough and margarines and shortenings.

So now you know a little about the bad fats, what about the good and why you should care?

HEALTHY FATS

It's amazing how many clients I work with who are afraid to eat anything that contains fat. Recently I was working with a women named Jan. Jan came to me claiming to be overweight. I told her I didn't see it, but she insisted she needed to lose 15 pound. She had just finished another stint on a diet program that has you watch your wait (hint, hint on the name of the diet) and was upset that she was not able to lose her last 15 pounds. I began to introduce Jan to a few of the key foods that help promote healthy weight loss and right away she wanted to know the fat content of these foods. I explained to Jan that there are healthy fats and bad fats and the ones I wanted her to eat would actually be helping to promote healthy weight lose. Like Jan, many North Americans have a bad habit of looking at nutritional labels to help make decisions. The problem with nutrition labels is that most of them are distorted towards foods that have very little nutritional value and therefore only offer empty calories. A nutritional label based on a whole, plant-based food is far different and offers your body quality sources of *The Big Three* including fat. So when Jan took a look at the nutritional label of the bag of sesame seeds I wanted her to start including in her diet, right away she looked at the fat content.

What makes the fat content in sesame seeds a healthier option compared to the saturated fat found in a steak or the trans fats found in the crackers you may enjoy?

Healthy fats come in the form of essential fatty acids. Essential means every human being needs sufficient amounts of these fats for optimal health. The body manufactures most of the fats it needs, except omega 3 and omega 6 fats, which are essential fatty acids and need to come from the foods you eat. These fats are vital for human nutrition and improve your body's ability to deal with internal and external stresses. Fat is everywhere in your body. Your brain is roughly 2/3 fat, an outer layer of fat protects your nerves and your body is covered in a layer of fat to help maintain your core body temperature. Whole food sources of omega 3 and 6 essential fatty acids are found primarily in seeds, nuts and avocados.

When you become aware of the different ways your body uses fat, it becomes quite clear how incorporating the healthy sources in your diet can improve your quality of life.

Getting a healthy dose of omega 3 and 6 essential fatty acids on a daily basis will support your ideal weight loss, improve your brain function, allowing for increase productivity and enhanced imagination, repair and strengthen hair, soften and beautify your skin, as well as ensure your metabolism is running optimally, and aid in the reduction of inflammation.

The recipe section of *e3 for LIFE* will show you how to incorporate healthier sources of fat into your diet without any restrictions from eating the foods you love. Once you try a few recipes, you will have no more excuses or desire to reach for foods that are rich in saturated and trans fats.

PROTEIN

Proteins are complex molecules made up of chains of amino acids. All together there are 20 amino acids. Eleven of them you already produce inside your body, which means the other 9 you have to get from the foods you choose to eat. What is it called when you find a food that has all 20 essential amino acids? It is called a complete protein. Some of the most popular sources of food which are commonly known as complete proteins are red meat and eggs, but are they really that healthy for you?

Protein is best known for its role in the formation and repair of muscle and bone. Do you remember what Popeye's favorite food was? Spinach! When Popeye would eat his spinach, he always found a little extra muscle and strength to get the job done, whether it was saving Olive Oyl or fighting off Brutus. However, protein has many other vital functions, such as insulin management, immune system regeneration and mineral transportation support.

Protein digestibility is important for your ability to maintain optimal health. I work with several clients who suffer from pH imbalances, which lead to a number of unwanted ailments. Your pH is the balance between acid and alkaline within your body. The more acidic you are the more damage you are causing your body on a cellular level. The initial impact of this damage may arise in the form of fatigue, weight gain or sleep deprivation, but the long term effects are much more severe. If you leave acidity too long, you cause significant stress on the body's ability to function optimally and if prolonged can cause your immune system to weaken and open the door to any number of ailments and disease such as cancer, heart disease, obesity and diabetes. I know this effect first hand. I lived off of antacid medication for three years when I was ill. Everything I ate created more and more acid, which left me feeling very sick. It was when I began reducing my meat intake and began including healthier sources of plant-based proteins, that I was able to stop using antacids to feel better. Protein creates acid. The heavier the protein, the more acid it will create. Finding protein sources that are both complete proteins and lower acid-forming sources will ensure you live a long and healthy life.

What is the ideal way to consume protein? Protein in its raw form is the ideal way to consume it. This is because raw protein is less acid-forming and easier on the body to digest. When you choose to get your protein from meat, dairy and processed foods such as breads, pastas or crackers, you are eating protein that has been compromised by being refined, altered and transform in some way. Another important point to be aware of is once you heat your food you alter the protein structure and make it more acid-forming. Many of my clients have experienced amazing health improvements when eating a whole-food, plant-based source of protein, which I consider to be the ideal way of ensuring you receive the protein nourishment you need.

One of my favorite ways to spend time is working with clients who grew up eating meat as their main source of protein. I know first hand what eating meat at every meal is like because it was how I grew up as well. One of my first clients I ever had the chance to work with was Joe. Joe, who was 45 when he came to me, was overweight, lacked energy and struggled with many digestive ailments including severe heartburn. I asked Joe during our very first session what his main source of protein was. He explained to me that he grew up eating meat at almost every meal and that was his main source of protein. With a sad voice, I recall Joe explaining to me how if he did not have a piece of meat on his plate he would not know where to get his protein from. There was a real sense of defeat in his voice because his lack of knowledge left him feeling scared and vulnerable. The breaking point for Joe came during our second session when he explained to me that he was just told he had high cholesterol and his doctor wanted him to change his diet to avoid becoming diabetic. I could relate to Joe because when I was 26, I was told the same thing and was overweight, battling high cholesterol, living off prescription drugs for my excessive heartburn and pre-diabetic.

"Adam, if I don't eat meat or chicken for dinner, I won't feel like I am feeding myself well."

I told Joe not to worry, we would get him on track very quickly and with ease. What is it that I shared with Joe that later allowed him to reduce his cholesterol levels to acceptable numbers within two months and gave him back control over his own health? I told him what I already told you, eat raw forms of plant based protein and reduce your intake of meat, dairy and refined foods. Raw forms of plant based protein are not as hard to find or consume as you might be thinking. Here are a few of my main sources, which can easily be added into your daily diet without any restrictions.

My number one protein source is hemp seeds. I eat about 6 tablespoons everyday. Sprinkled on my cereal for breakfast, in my smoothies, on my salad or soup for lunch. I even make amazing cookies using hemp seeds, which you can find on my website at www.PowerofFood.com. Other raw forms of protein I consume include flax seeds, sprouts, dark green leafy vegetables like kale and spinach, quinoa and almonds. I promise you that if you include more whole food sources of protein into your diet, you will experience a shift in your energy levels in a matter of days.

CARBOHYDRATES

Carbohydrates are your main source of fuel because they turn into sugar faster then fats and proteins. There are two types of carbohydrates – simple and complex – and both are made up of sugar, fiber and starch. It is your choice of carbohydrates, depending on what you eat, that will determine if you are eating a simple or complex carbohydrate. For example, if you eat commercial bread, pasta, cereals, cookies or crackers, you are eating a simple carbohydrate. This is because when whole grains are refined, the majority of nutritional value is removed, leaving a simplified version of what it used to be. This simplified version of food is what a typical North American diet relies on, therefore leaving the body starving for energy all day long.

When we eat simple carbohydrates we get a quick burst of insulin injected into our blood stream to help transport the glucose to our cells in order to produce energy, but that burst is short lived.

I want to introduce you to Jenny. Jenny came to my *Power of Food* presentation at the Vancouver Wellness Show in 2009 and discovered that I too had suffered like she was now suffering with low energy, high cholesterol and weight management issues. Right after the presentation Jenny asked if I would coach her. I agreed to take her on and enrolled Jenny in one of my *Power of Food Nutrition Coaching Programs.*

During our first session I knew right away Jenny was consuming all the wrong carbohydrates. Her diet consisted mainly of processed foods such as bread, pasta, cereals, crackers, cookies and other baked goods. Jenny was very much like many of my clients. She lacked knowledge on how carbohydrates really worked and was frustrated and angry that she didn't know what to do.

I introduced Jenny to the world of whole foods. We focused on her carbohydrate intake since she had recently experienced failure on a popular diet that restricted her carbohydrate intake. I told her that when you restrict your body of carbohydrates you could be causing a lot more damage than good. The key, I explained, was to remove the simple, refined carbohydrates and bring in the complex carbohydrates from whole, plant-based foods. These are the carbohydrates that will provide abundant energy all day long.

The main difference between simple carbohydrates and complex carbohydrates are their nutrient content. Is your morning cereal providing you with simple or complex carbohydrates? The truth is there are very few packaged cereals that have not been heavily refined, this applies to oatmeal as well, and therefore have lost most of their nutritional value. This means when you eat your breakfast cereal, you are fueling yourself with sugar. That is why you have no energy by 10 am. Then at 10 am you eat a few crackers or a muffin – again refined grains with little nutrient – so another burst of sugar and then another crash before your lunch. Now it's 12 pm and you decide to grab a bagel or a wrap from the local restaurant. What is the bagel or wrap made of? Refined grains once again and now your sugar goes up and crashes down again. Then you get to 2 pm and can't figure out why you have no energy and feel like crap.

Jenny related to this daily sequence of eating refined carbohydrates and was very keen to learn what type of complex carbohydrates she could eat. I introduce Jenny to many of the whole foods I discovered to provide me with abundant energy all day long. I showed Jenny how to use quinoa, whole oat groats, amaranth, flax seeds and hemp seeds.

I recommend she start adding a tablespoon or two of each of these foods during her morning breakfast. I also got Jenny to take a container with a mix of these 5 whole foods to work and add a few scoops to whatever she was eating for lunch. Jenny liked the idea that she did not need to restrict herself in what to eat, only that she had to add something healthy to what she already liked to eat. This is the *e3 for LIFE* main message – NO RESTRICTIONS. Jenny found this easy and before long she was bringing healthier whole foods into everything she ate and providing her body with abundant nutrients to build energy from. Within three weeks Jenny was feeling fantastic. She had more energy, she lost 7 pounds, without restrictions, and she was craving more whole foods and less refined foods. Jenny called me up one morning to thank me and this is what she said:

"Adam, I can't thank you enough. You have helped me in so many ways. Not only do I no longer have constant food cravings, but also I feel more in control of my life. You made it easy for me to be happy."

I remember her call like it was yesterday. To this day Jenny calls me and emails me every few weeks to tell me how she is doing and to check in.

In the end it is all about what complex carbohydrates you add to the foods you already like to eat. This is your starting point so that you begin to fuel yourself with the energy-rich carbohydrates without restrictions. Once you begin eating more whole foods such as quinoa and hemp seeds, you will stop struggling with energy and begin managing your weight with ease. Yes it is that simple.

THE BIG THREE CONCLUSION

You have now discovered that a large potion of the North American diet is made up of foods that are based on what was once a whole food, such as a whole grain of wheat, which is then turned into flour. This flour has very little nutritional value left. And the other part of our diets are made of excessive meat and dairy consumption, which is very heavy on the body. Why should you care? If you eat bread, pasta, cereal, cookies or crackers, along with a lot of meat and dairy, you need to care, because your body is starving for healthy fats, high quality proteins and complex carbohydrates. Chances are

you already have trouble with your weight, are over-stressed and suffer from the mid-afternoon crashes. The more your body starves for nutrients, the higher risk you have of attaining cancer, diabetes or heart disease. You have the choice – it's time to begin taking back control over your own health.

The recipe section of *e3 for LIFE* will provide you with over 60 recipes on how to introduce healthier sources of fats, proteins and carbohydrates without any restrictions to your diet. The key is to begin by adding nutrient-rich sources of *The Big Three* and becoming more aware of how you feel after you eat these foods. I promise you that if you pay closer attention to how you feel, you will begin to seek out healthier options, because they make you feel so good and provide abundant energy, which is the quickest way to gage your results.

TASTE BUD BLUES :(

Before I introduce you to all the tasty and nutritious recipes to try, there is a little unfinished business we must attend to. I want to go back to the farm for a moment. Do you remember what happens to the wheat the farmer harvests from his field? That's right, it gets turned into flour. And as mentioned earlier, there is very little nutritional value left in that flour by the time it gets to you. So what about the taste?

What do you suppose flour tastes like?

When was the last time you licked some flour? Not too tasty right? So in order to make the bread, cracker, cereal or cookies taste good what do you think food manufactures need to add? That's right, they pump it full of additives. What do you suppose are the top three additives in commercial food? **Salt, Sugar and Fat.**

When you think about eating whole foods what comes to mind?

It won't taste good.

Everything is going to be bland.

There is no way my children will eat it.

Do any of these come up for you?

From the minute we are born, the majority of North Americans are introduced to salt, sugar and fat. These happen to be the three most added ingredients in most processed and refined foods, and making up the majority of our diets. They also happen to be three of the most damaging ingredients to our health. From obesity to diabetes, heart disease to high blood pressure, salt, sugar and fat have overtaken our grocery store shelves. Why is it that our taste buds have been taken hostage right from a young age? Because it sells more food, it's that simple.

Your taste buds are constantly searching for salt, sugar and fat and unless you feed that addiction, your taste buds will surely let you know. How will they let you know? By sending a pain or pleasure signal to your brain. Your taste buds inform your thought process whether to be happy or not. *This stuff taste bland, I can't eat this, there is no flavor*, are just a few examples of how your taste buds sabotage your ability to eat healthier foods.

Our mind will do anything to avoid pain and anything to gain pleasure. Salt, sugar and fat equal pleasure. Eating a diet rich in whole foods is a natural detox. Not only will you begin to flush toxic waste from your body, but your taste buds will begin to be weaned off of their sugar, salt and fat dependency. Once this occurs, you will realize that healthy food actually has a natural flavor that is very pleasing to the pallet.

If you were to add up every ingredient in a particular commercial packaged food item, in most cases, salt, sugar and fat would list 2, 3 and 4 right behind the wheat. Let's take a look at sugar as an example. There are many names used for sugar. They include:

Brown sugar

Corn syrup

Demerara Sugar

Dextrose

Free Flowing Brown Sugars

Fructose

Galactose

Glucose

High Fructose Corn Syrup

Honey

Invert Sugar

Lactose

Malt

Maltodextrin

Maltose

Maple syrup

Molasses

Powdered or confectioner's sugar

Rice Syrup

Sucrose

Sugar (granulated)

Treacle

Turbinado sugar

Why so many names? Because Food manufacturers try to add as much sugar as possible without us knowing. It's simple business practices. They know the more sugar they can add, the more we will buy. The truth is, salt, sugar and fat are the only ways to keep us eating commercial food products; otherwise, there is no taste and therefore no sales.

Not only are salt, sugar and fat found in almost every commercial product, but food manufacturers also add a large amount of flavor enhancers to ensure you enjoy every last bite. A good example of a flavor enhancer that is used quite often is monosodium glutamate. Have you ever heard of MSG? MSG is a neurotoxin that is used to hook your taste buds to what you are eating. Many studies have linked monosodium glutamate to obesity.

Most of the additives used to enhance flavor are fat soluble, meaning they are stored inside your fat cells for long period of time until one day you walk into the doctor's office and wonder why you now have diabetes or cancer. It is unfortunate, but most of my clients don't come to me until they are already sick or have children who are. The key to your health is to be preventative and that is what *e3 for LIFE* can help you achieve.

What about shelf life? Most grocery stores will not carry food on their shelves unless it lasts at least six months without going bad. In order to ensure adequate shelf life what do food manufactures now have to add? Right again, preservatives. Once again more chemicals are added to your food in order to ensure they last on the shelves. Just like with additives, the major problem with preservatives is that they too are fat soluble and are stored up in your fat cells with every bite.

Wheat is just one example of this mass processing of our whole foods. That is why *e3 for LIFE* focuses on making it easy for you to introduce whole, plant foods into your diet without restricting yourself from the foods you love. I will introduce you to the system that will allow you to do this, but first we must talk about meat and why it falls in with the other type of food that is not whole and that is processed.

MEAT & DAIRY

Meat and dairy unfortunately fall into the category of processed because of modern agriculture. Now I know what many of you may be thinking, *here goes Adam talking about how I should not eat meat and become a vegetarian.* The truth is I still eat some meat and I am not telling you what you should or should not do, I am only here to present a picture for you to make informed decisions, to take action for your own health.

I grew up eating meat at every meal. Just like Joe who I described earlier, if there was not a piece of meat on my plate, I had no idea where my iron or protein was coming from. That also worked for dairy. If I was not drinking milk, I had no clue where I would get my calcium. Does this sound familiar to you? Right from a young age many of us are indoctrinated on the supposed benefits of meat and dairy as healthy sources of nutrients. Unfortunately with modern agriculture and over-consumption, this is not so accurate anymore. The discussion around meat is worthy of a full book on its own and that is not my intention with *e3 for LIFE* so I have provided you with plenty of references in the back for you to explore the subject further if you wish. For the sake of our discussion let's spend a few minutes exploring meat production and why I include it with processed food and not a whole food.

As I mentioned earlier I define meat as all chicken, eggs, dairy, red meat, fish, pork, turkey, and lamb. I put them all together because they all have very similar modern production practices. With that I mean that they are produced using heavy amounts of antibiotic, hormones, poor quality feed and poor quality living conditions. Included here is also the addition of a hormone many animals secrete when they go through fear. When an animal is held captive and/or slaughtered, the animals secrete a fear hormone, which ends up being transferred to the human who consumes it.

I am not suggesting that you stop eating meat, but I do suggest you become aware of the impact excessive meat consumption is having on your health and the health of your loved ones. I still eat meat as I mentioned, but now I do my best to consume only animal products that are certified organic or ones where I know the source personally. There are no excuses with this one. There are too many local or certified organic options available, especially in major city centers across North America.

The other issue around meat is that we tend to over-consume it. Not only in our daily consumption of it, but in our portion sizes as well. Most meats tend to be excessive in their nutrient content and are quite heavy on the body to digest. The average portion size for a piece of red meat should be no bigger then a deck of cards or the palm of your hand.

When was the last time you sat down for a steak that big? Not likely. I know my steaks used to be around twice that size. Think about your digestive system for a minute. As you will learn in a few minutes one of its main functions it to pull nutrients from the food you eat. If your body is always filled with heavy meats, it is very tough for your digestive system to pull it apart and break it down to use the nutrients efficiently. How do you normally feel after eating a steak? Full, satisfied, sleepy? All that energy going to digestion is now leaving the rest of your body vulnerable to fighting disease and illness. When consuming whole, plant-based foods you will discover ample amounts of high quality, nutrient rich sources that are easier on the body to digest and provide a boost to your immune system instead of depriving as often found in a heavy meat diet.

Now you can see a better picture as to why you may be having trouble losing weight or suffering from fatigue and low energy. As North Americans, so many of us over consume meat products while at the same time rely on foods that have very little nutritional value. This means we spend too much energy on digestion while simultaneously experiencing energy crashes over and over again. That is why we have so many food cravings and continue to reach for the same foods over and over again. These foods provide pleasure because of their sugar, salt and fat. Every bite provides a rise in your serotonin levels, the pleasure chemical released by your brain, and leaves you coming back for more. In addition we are storing all the hormones, antibiotics, fat soluble additives and preservatives within our bodies contributing to our obesity, diabetes and cancer. Now it's time to make a choice. Do you want to keep feeling the way you do? OR are you ready to experience a healthier more vibrant you?

If you are ready, it is time to discover the system I created that will make it easy for you to gain back control over your own health with ease.

SUCCESS SYSTEM #1 – 80/20 RULE

I want you to take 30 seconds and imagine you were stranded on a desert island. Take these few second and think of the one food you could not live without. What is that one favorite food that you would most like to have with you? I know for me it is without a doubt hemp seeds. Not too long ago I would have said shortbread cookies, but now it is hemp seeds.

Why do you think I would get you to engage your favorite food?

The reason for engaging your favorite food is to acknowledge the foods you love to eat and celebrate them. Living a healthy and happy life has nothing to do with restrictions or eliminating anything from your life or diet. It has everything to do with celebrating the foods you love while at the same time bringing in foods that offer abundant nutritional value. That is where the *80/20 Rule* of eating comes in.

My system for gaining back control over my own health started when I came up with the concept of the *80/20 Rule*. Have you heard of the *80/20 Rule* before? Yes, it has been used in other scenarios, such as

in business where the *80/20 Rule* is know as: *80% of your sales come from 20% of your clients*. The *80/20 Rule* I created is a system for eating where 80% of the time I eat foods that offer me superior nutritional value in the form of whole, plant based foods, while the other 20% I can eat whatever I want, whenever I want.

In North America what is our main problem with the *80/20 Rule*?

WE HAVE THE *80/20 RULE* BACKWARDS!

This means that 80% of what many North Americans are eating on a daily basis is based on heavily-refined, over-processed foods that offer very little in the way of nutritional value. With our digestive systems constantly in distress due to our lack of nutrient rich foods, the 20% of what we eat that actually offers nutrients for health do not get used properly.

If I told you that as of today you should follow the 80/20 Rule and eat 80% of your diet based on nuts, seeds, grains, legumes, fruits and vegetable, how would you feel? If you said frustrated or confused as to where to begin, you are not alone. Many of my clients have mentioned that 80% is too daunting.

I don't know where to begin.

How is that possible?

That won't be very much fun.

The great news is that you do not need to be at 80% right now. Through all my nutritional coaching, I have discovered that it is easiest to provide a smaller number to being with and through reaching this number, 80% become easy to attain.

THE MAGIC NUMBER

There is a magic number one must attain in order to begin to feel the full benefits of eating healthier foods.

The Magic Number is 51%.

51% is your starting point, not 80%. The key is to get to the point where you eat whole foods for 51% of your diet. Think of it in terms of trying to swim up river. If you are constantly trying to swim up river, you are no doubt going to drown, it is just a matter of time, just like it is happening with your health and the lack of nutrients you currently may or may not be provid-

ing. At 51% you begin to get your head above water and begin to feel what it is like to stop fighting against the current and being shifting your course to eventually flow with ease down the river. From this point, your body and mind begin to assist you in your ability to gain strength to where you are eventually swimming down river without any struggle. It is at this point that you will have set up a system for eating that will make the 80% happen automatically. I am happy to tell you that there is a 3-step process that will make it easy for you to achieve *The Magic Number.*

3 STEPS TO REACHING 51%

Step 1. What are the ideal foods for reaching 51% with ease.

Step 2. How to use these foods on a daily basis without any restrictions to your current diet.

Step 3. How to use these foods creatively to begin coasting down river to 80%.

You already know Step 1. These are whole, plant based foods and you will learn more about them during the recipe section. Step 2 is all about bringing whole foods into your daily life without any restrictions whatsoever. This is the crucial stage where you only add more nuts, seeds, grains, legumes, fruits and vegetables into your current diet to increase the nutritional value for what you already like to eat. No changes or alterations to your diet in anyway is the key to you reaching Step 3. Just adding a tablespoon or two of certain nuts, seeds, grains, legumes, fruits and vegetables to whatever it is you already love to eat without restrictions will begin to help you control your blood sugar, reduce cravings and provide you with sustained energy. Sounds too simple? That's because it is simple! Too many of us look for the miracle pill to get healthier. The reality is, just adding in healthier, nutrient rich whole foods into your current diet, will make a HUGE difference to the way you look and feel. I guarantee you will feel stronger and more energized within a matter of days.

I once had a gentleman at one of my Power of Food workshops ask me:

So, Adam, what you are telling me is if I add hemp seeds to my Big Mac I will be healthier?

What do you think the answer is?

YES, there is a large amount of nutritional value in hemp seeds and not a whole lot in the Big Mac. The only thing you get from a Big Mac is a huge amount of useless calories, so of course the answer is YES.

Once you bring in whole foods into your daily routine without altering your diet in any other way, you will begin to provide your body and mind with nutrients you've been starving for. This will begin a process where you will start to crave more of the good and less of the bad, which will help you naturally and easily begin to experience a shift in your health.

It is amazing how the body works. I grew up all meat and dairy and that was where I got my protein, iron and calcium. As soon as I began to eat whole, plant-based sources of protein, iron and calcium, my body craved them more. If you only feed your body one source for its nutrients, then that is what it will crave most, because it needs them to survive. When you introduce healthier sources of the same nutrients, your body will seek them out and shift your food cravings to a healthier state.

One crucial point I need to share with you is to ensure that you take care of yourself first. If you try and bring the *80/20 Rule* into the lives of your loved one, you may run into frustration and opposition. The key is to do it for yourself first and then those you love most will automatically join in, because they will see how great you look and how much energy you have.

Step 3 is all about taking whole foods to the next level. By getting creative using nuts, seeds, grains, legumes, fruits and vegetables, you will reach the optimal 80% of the *80/20 Rule* with ease. The recipe section of *e3 for LIFE* will give you the guidance you need to make this a reality.

e3 for LIFE makes reaching *The Magic Number* of 51% realistic in a short period of time, while guiding you to then achieving the optimal 80% whole food diet. To stress the importance of the *80/20 Rule* I would like share with you what I discovered about our digestive system, which will make it easier for you to maximize the results you desire. It is through your digestive system that your ability to heal is revealed.

BONUS – POWER OF FOOD JOURNAL

Would you like a simple system for tracking your daily results in reaching *The Magic Number*? Below you will find the *Power of Food Daily Journal* I designed for my personal *Power of Food Nutrition Coaching* clients. This food journal makes it easy to track your daily progress.

HOW IT WORKS

Each day list everything you eat. For example: if you eat a bowl of cereal or oatmeal you would place an x beside it. If you add hemps seeds, ground flax seeds and quinoa to your cereal you will now have three checkmarks. Now for lunch you have a ham and cheese sandwich. The bread would get an x because it is refined and the ham and cheese would each get an x because those are also under the processed side of food. Now it's all about what you add. For each vegetable you put into your sandwich you get a checkmark. Spinach?

Checkmark. Tomato slices? Checkmark. What about adding some ground almonds or more hemp seeds? The more whole foods you add, the more checkmarks you receive. Do you get the idea? You still get to eat your ham and cheese sandwich, but just add more nutrient-rich whole foods to increase your ability to reach 51%. It's that easy.

Feel free to print off a few copies from your *e3 for LIFE* book to get you started. You can also visit www.PowerofFood.com to order the full version of your *80/20 Rule Power of Food Daily Journal* to track your daily progress.

You can even sign up under the member's area at www.PowerofFood.com to track your *Power of Food Daily Journal* progress online.

Adam Hart's Power of Food.com

Daily Food Journal

Date:

Today I ate (list everything you ate or drank today)	Time I ate or drank	Whole Food ✔ Refined Food X
	Total X	**Total ✔**
Did you make it above 51% today?	**My Daily % today is**	**%**

If you have more ✔ then X you are above 51%. What was your % for the day?

DIGESTIVE HEALTH

In order to understand the importance of eating whole foods we must take a quick look at your digestive system. The digestive system was my starting point back when I was overweight and pre-diabetic. I wanted to understand what high cholesterol meant without having to rely on prescription drugs. Within a couple of years I had read hundreds of health books that mention the importance of digestive health for optimal vitality. Many of these books were very scientific and as you can imagine, very confusing to read. Being persistent with wanting to take control over my own health, I continued researching and began to notice a pattern. Without getting too scientific, I realized that there are two main functions of the digestive system.

Do you ever think about your digestive system?

Or do you only think about it when you are bloated, gassy, constipated or in discomfort?

Many of us don't give credit to the power within our own digestive system and its ability to help us maintain our optimal health.

DS FUNCTION #1

The first main function of your digestive system is to pull out nutrients from the foods you choose to eat. I know it sound simple, but this fact is extremely important. Think about it for a minute: everything you put into your mouth and swallow, your digestive system uses in one way or another. The digestive system pulls nutrients out of the food you eat and feeds it to your trillions of cells to provide them with health. So if your diet mainly consists of over-processed, refined foods, what nutrients are there to be pulled out? Not much, leaving your cells starving for health. Eating whole, plant based foods offers abundant nutritional power, giving your digestive system ample nutrients to distribute to your cells, allowing them to perform necessary functions to keep you feeling fantastic. Would you like to feel fantastic everyday?

DS FUNCTION #2

The second main function of your digestive system is to kill off bad bacteria.

Did you know that you have both good and bad bacteria in your body right now?

This fact is very important when wanting to cure dis-ease within the body. Throughout the entire digestive process you have both good and bad bacteria impacting your digestive flora. The more good you have, the healthier you will be, it's that simple. I am now going to reveal to you the most important piece of information of the entire *e3 for LIFE* book:

Over 70% of your immune system lies within your digestive system.

What is your immune system meant to do? That's right, keep you healthy.

So wouldn't it make sense that eating foods that offer higher nutritional value would benefit your immune health? You bet it does. I contribute the strengthening of my immune system to my diet shifting from 20/80 based on heavily-refined foods to 80/20 based on eating whole foods.

The discovery of my digestive system and its two main functions turned out to be the single most important step in my ability to lose weight, reverse my pre-diabetic state and attain abundant energy. I am sure it can do the same for you if you are ready.

WHAT'S IN YOUR CALORIES?

I really do want to share with you my amazing *Power of Food* recipes, but there is one more item we must clear up before we begin enjoying some of the scrumptious delights waiting for you on the coming pages. I was walking the aisles at my local grocery store recently when I noticed a young girl reading a nutritional label on a box of cereal. She must have been no older then 13 years old. I was surprised to see her reading the label and could also see she was frustrated. I walked over to her and introduced myself and asked her what she was looking for on the label. She told me her name was Molly and what she said next rang very loud and clear. It was the same thing so many of my clients have told me in the past and continue to struggle with daily. Molly said she was looking at how many calories were in each portion. Immediately alarm bells went off in my head, as I knew Molly was a victim of the *North American Calorie Confusion Syndrome.* I just made that name up, but it works.

Molly was only 13 and she was already trying to count calories. I knew this would set her up for a lifetime of frustration if I did not provide her with some sound advice as to what calories truly are and how to use food for its real value. Essentially I told Molly what I am about to share with you below. Once in a while I see Molly around my local grocery store and she is always quick to come over and say hello with a very big smile. I feel so fortunate to be a role model to young kids as they suffer just as much as adults when it comes to being confused about food. Here is what I explained to Molly.

Not all calories are created equal. It's great that you might be trying to lose a few pounds and therefore counting your calorie intake, but to succeed with *e3 for LIFE*, it is crucial to be aware of the fact that not all calories are created equal.

I get asked all the time, *but Adam, how many calories are in that?* It's not the calories that count. It's what is in the calories that make the difference to your health.

In order to explain this better, let's take a quick look at calories.

Each calorie is defined as a unit of energy and your body needs a certain amount of energy each day to maintain essential body function. With every bite you take, the food you eat is providing you with the energy you need to perform daily actions. If you go over your needed amount of calories each day, and you're not a very active person, you will eventually gain weight. The average adult should look to consume 2000 to 2500 calories per day. In North America we tend to eat on the opposite end of the scale, somewhere in the range of 3000 to 5000 calories daily. That's a lot of extra calories being stored in your body and a major cause of weight gain. These calories should be made up of foods that offer superior nutrition, but this is where we get into the problem. Most of the calories we consume are heavily-refined, over-processed and void of essential nutrients. This means that when we reach for the box of crackers or a bag of chips we are fueling our bodies far differently than if we were to reach for hemp seeds, or a bag of raw almonds.

Energy is supplied through the foods

you eat which are made up of the essential building blocks of all life. These essential building blocks are *The Big Three* as discussed earlier, fats, proteins and carbohydrates. The more you eat whole, plant-based foods, the more your calories will supply you with quality proteins, essential fatty acids and complex carbohydrates, providing the vital nutrients required for your optimal health. With so many people focused on calorie counting, it's no wonder there is so much confusion as to why we keep failing when trying to achieve our desired health goals.

Processed Foods = Empty Calories =
Fatigue & Weight Gain

Whole Foods = Calories Your Body Will
Use = Abundant Energy & Vitality

The more you eat over-processed, refined foods you can be sure your calorie intake will be comprised of simple sugars which will only leave you weak, fatigued, continually craving more food and susceptible to weight gain.

Eventually, if you stay the course with *e3 for LIFE*, what you will find is that you will be able to manage your weight better,

feel more energy on a daily basis as well as find the ability to deal with stress with ease. My personal experience was that after I added more whole foods into my daily diet (Step 1 from the *80/20 Rule*), I immediately began to desire the positive health effects they provided. This allowed me to experience an easy shift from 20/80 on the refined side to 51% on the whole foods side (Step 2 of the *80/20 Rule*), to where now I eat nuts, seeds, grains, legumes, fruits and vegetables for 80% of my diet (Step 3). That is what *e3 for LIFE* will help you achieve without any restrictions and with ease.

I now want to introduce you to some of my favorite *Power of Food* recipes. These recipes will make it easy for you to shift your diet towards the optimal *80/20 RULE*.

WHAT YOU CAN LOOK FORWARD TO

All of my recipes are vegan or vegetarian with a large amount being raw. I do not talk about eating vegan, vegetarian or raw in *e3 for LIFE* because I feel that many of us are not ready for this transition, but do want to eat healthier. My approach is to first help you move away from a heavy processed food diet and begin bringing in healthier whole, plant-based foods into your life. Once you have a good handle on what whole foods are (Step 1), how to use them daily (Step 2) and how to use them creatively (Step 3), then going vegan, vegetarian or raw are all options I support strongly.

Every recipe provided I created to be simple for you to try and taste great. All of my recipes offer you a huge amount of nutritional value for every bite while saving you time and energy to get out and play. By trying these recipes and using them daily, you will move from eating a diet of 51% to 80% whole foods with ease. Get ready to feel amazing!

Look for the special bonus feature throughout the recipe section where I share with you some of the key features of my favorite super foods.

JUMP START GRANOLA

INGREDIENTS (MAKES 4 CUPS)

1 cup steel-cut oats

1 cup sunflower seeds

1/2 cup unhulled sesame seeds

1-1/2 teaspoon cinnamon

1/4 teaspoon nutmeg

1/4 teaspoon sea salt

1/4 cup natural honey

2 tablespoon apple juice

HOW TO PREPARE

Preheat your oven to 300°F. Mix all your dry ingredients in a bowl. In a separate container, blend all your liquid ingredients until you reach a smooth texture. Add the liquid ingredients to your dry ingredients and mix well. Spread the mixture on a baking tray. Bake for 40 minutes. Let the granola cool and then break it up into desired size pieces. Store your cereal in an airtight container.

RECIPE TIP

Add any number of organic dried fruits to increase the flavor and sweetness. Even better would be to top off your bowl of granola with some fresh seasonal berries.

MORNING BOOSTER JUICE

INGREDIENTS (MAKES 2 CUPS OF JUICE)

1 tablespoon flax oil

1/4 cup water

3 tablespoon cashews, ground

2 tablespoon hemp seeds

1 cup almond milk or rice milk

1/2 cup spinach

1/2 cup fruit – choose any seasonal berries

OPTIONAL ADDITIONS

Add a 1/4 cup of cooked whole oat groats or quinoa. This will make the smoothie a little thicker and enhance the taste and nutritional content.

HOW TO PREPARE

Place all ingredients together into a blender and blend. Add more liquid as needed to reach your desired consistency.

SPECIAL WEBSITE FEATURE

Visit **www.PowerofFood.com** to watch a video on how to prepare this recipe.

RECIPE TIP

Try making double the amount and having the second portion for a lunch or snack.

RISE & SHINE CEREAL

INGREDIENTS (MAKES 1 BOWL)

1/4 cup of your favorite cereal

1 tablespoon flax seed, ground

1 tablespoon hemp seeds

1 tablespoon sunflower seeds

1 tablespoon sesame seeds, ground

1/2 cup cooked or soaked whole oat groats or quinoa

1 teaspoon natural honey

1 tablespoon organic raisins or cranberries

1 cup rice milk or almond milk

HOW TO PREPARE

Place all your ingredients into a bowl and enjoy.

RECIPE TIP

Take the same recipe (without the milk and honey) in a container to work and enjoy as a snack or for lunch.

Super Food

Whole Oat Power

Whole oat groats are a great source of fiber, complex carbohydrates, calcium and phosphorous as well as a high source of quality protein.

HOW TO USE

You can cook whole oat groats the same as rice, but I prefer to soak them. They are easy to soak and this ensures you maintain their full nutritional value. Rinse your whole oats thoroughly by running them under fresh water. For every cup of whole oat groats you soak, you will need 2 cups of water. Leave them soaking overnight. In the morning, rinse your grains with fresh water and serve. No heating necessary.

SUGGESTIONS FOR DAILY USE

Breakfast: Sprinkle 4 tablespoons into your morning cereal or smoothie. You can even top a few tablespoons with fresh seasonal fruit and a little natural honey.

Lunch/Snack: Add 2 tablespoons into your salad, soup or sandwich.

Dinner: Here is a bonus recipe as an example of how easy it is to use grains in creative ways. Cut open the tops of 2 red peppers. Place in oven at 350 for 25 minutes. Once baked, stuff with mixture of soaked whole oat groats, ground almonds and some dried cranberries. It's easy to add them to any meal and enjoy a boost of health in every bite.

HOW TO STORE

Uncooked whole oat groats can be stored in a dark airtight container. Once cooked, whole oat groats should be stored in your fridge. I tend to prepare 1 to 2 cups per week and store in my fridge for quick, daily access to add to the foods I love to eat.

SHELF LIFE

Uncooked in the cupboard for up to 6 months; when cooked in the fridge up to 5 days.

MOOO OVER MOOO MILK

INGREDIENTS
(MAKES 2 CUPS OF ALMOND MILK)

1 cup almonds, soaked

1/4 cup pitted dates, chopped & soaked

1 teaspoon natural honey

1/2 teaspoon pure vanilla extract

1 cheese cloth

HOW TO PREPARE

In two separate bowls soak your almonds in two cups of water and dates in 1-1/2 cups of water overnight. Rinse almonds in the morning. Place all the ingredients, including the water the dates soaked in, into a food processor or blender. As it blends, keep adding more water until the liquid becomes the desired consistency. Place the liquid into a cheese cloth and squeeze out your almond milk over a large bowl.

RECIPE TIP

Once you have removed as much milk as possible, place your milk into a glass container and store in the refrigerator. Almond milk will last for 3 to 4 days in the fridge. The leftover pulp may be stored in the freezer and used to make any num-

ber of delicious baked goods, as you will see with the Zucchini Nut Muffins recipe in the snack section of your *e3 for LIFE* recipes. You can even sprinkle some of the pulp over any recipe creation.

BANANA FLAX JACKS

INGREDIENTS (MAKES 6 PANCAKES)

1/4 cup ground flax seeds

1 tablespoon unground flax seeds

1 organic egg

1 cup rice milk or almond milk

1-1/2 cup buckwheat flour

1 tablespoon raw cane sugar

2 teaspoons baking powder

1/2 teaspoon baking soda

1/4 teaspoon Himalayan crystal salt

1 banana, sliced thin

1 teaspoon cinnamon

HOW TO PREPARE

Combine and mix all your dry ingredients into one bowl and all your wet ingredients into another except the banana. Add the wet into the dry bowl and mix. In a pan, place batter into hand-size portions and place a few slices of banana into the top side of each pancake. Cook over medium heat in a little coconut oil or butter until done. Garnish with the rest of your banana.

RECIPE TIP

Any leftovers are great as a snack for work or play. Try using a little almond butter or applesauce instead of maple syrup.

Super Food

Flax Power

There is so much nutritional value in this little seed. I consider flax the toothbrush of your intestines, cleansing you of unwanted toxins. Flax seed is best if ground to help release the soluble and insoluble forms of fiber. Once ground the essential fatty acid content coupled with a strong dose of fiber makes flax seeds a must for a healthy diet.

HOW TO USE

Flax seeds, like most other seeds, can be eaten raw, no heat or soaking required. Flax seeds are usually not consumed whole but rather ground since this allows for all their healthy benefits to be released and to enhance their nutrient absorption. Look at it this way – if you have the same flax seeds hanging around your fridge for more than 2 weeks, you need to find different ways to use them, because they are a vital factor in your ability to attain better health.

SUGGESTIONS FOR DAILY USE

Breakfast: Sprinkle 2 ground tablespoons into your cereal, smoothie or baked goods such as muffins and breads.

Lunch/Snack: Grind 2 tablespoons in a coffee grinder and spread on top of a sandwich or put into soups or salads.

Dinner: Grind some flax seeds and add into veggie burgers, over steamed vegetables or mixed into whatever you are eating; just do it, and increase the essential fatty acid content of every meal!

HOW TO STORE

Due to the high content of essential fatty acids contained in flax seeds, it is important to store your flax seeds in the fridge or freezer. Keep them stored in the door of your fridge for quick access.

SHELF LIFE

Ground seeds in fridge for up to 3 months; unground in freezer up to 6 months.

HUNGRY HUNGRY HUMMUS

INGREDIENTS (MAKES 4 CUPS)

2 cans chickpeas

1 tablespoon prepared mustard

3 tablespoons tahini

Juice from 2 fresh lemons

1/4 cup of rice milk or almond milk

1 teaspoon natural honey

1 large onion, diced

2 tablespoons fresh oregano

4 cloves garlic, minced

1 teaspoon Himalayan crystal salt

1 teaspoon fresh ground peppers

HOW TO PREPARE

Rinse your chickpeas and place them into a food processor with all your remaining ingredients. Purée all together and add more liquid to reach your desired consistency. Serve with organic corn chips or fresh whole grain crackers.

RECIPE TIP

Try boosting the nutritional value and flavor of your hummus by adding a variety of oils into the purée such as flax, sesame and hemp. If the garlic and onion are too potent to your taste buds raw, you can sauté the garlic and onions with teaspoon of olive oil and maple syrup over medium heat for 2 minutes.

Super Food

Chickpea Power

Chickpeas are a delicious burst of health – full of complex carbohydrates, lots of fiber, great source of quality protein as well as B vitamins, iron and many many more vitamins and essential minerals.

HOW TO USE

For canned beans, open and rinse with fresh water. For dried beans soak for 4 to 6 hours before cooking. This hydration helps to reduce cooking time. Strain water and place beans into a pot of fresh water and bring to a boil. Once boiled, reduce to a simmer until beans are soft, approx 45 minutes. Once done, strain, rinse and store in your fridge.

SUGGESTIONS FOR DAILY USE

Breakfast: Try adding 1/4 cup chickpea flour to replace 1/4 cup of your regular flour in any baking recipe or pancakes.

Lunch/Snack: How about adding chickpeas directly into your soups or salads? Why not spread a little Hungry Hungry Hummus on sprouted grain bread or crackers for a healthy kick to your afternoon?

Dinner: Chickpeas are amazing addition to vegetable burgers, stews or stir-fries. Don't forget their versatile use in many Indian dishes as well.

HOW TO STORE

Canned chickpeas will last for several years. Dried chickpeas should be stored in a dark place in an airtight container. Once cooked, chickpeas should be stored in the fridge. I tend to have two cans stocked for quick access throughout the week.

SHELF LIFE

Dried chickpeas in cupboard for up to 6 months; cooked or opened in your fridge for 4 days.

GLUTEN FREE
BROWN RICE WRAP

INGREDIENTS (MAKES 1 WRAP)

1 brown rice wrap

1 tablespoon tahini

1 avocado

1 tablespoon hemp seeds

handful of spinach

2 tablespoons ground almonds

HOW TO PREPARE

Place all your ingredients into the wrap and roll. That's an easy one.

RECIPE TIP

Get creative with these wraps. Try making an almond butter and jam wrap for a quick, healthy lunch or snack.

VEGGIETASTIC QUESADILLA

INGREDIENTS (MAKES 1 QUESADILLA)

1/2 onion, diced

1/2 red pepper, diced

1/2 cup spinach

2 cloves garlic, minced

2 brown rice wraps (gluten-free)

1/2 cup of organic cheese

1 tablespoon olive oil

2 tablespoons of hemp seeds

HOW TO PREPARE

Place a tablespoon of olive oil and a tablespoon of water into a large pan and set your stove top to low heat. Now place one brown rice wrap into the pan. Place all your ingredients evenly throughout the wrap and cover with a lid. Let the wrap cook slowly for a few minutes or until toppings are a little steamed. Place the second warp over top and bring your stove top to medium heat. Flip your wrap after a few minutes. Once the ingredients reach desired consistency, cut into four wedges and serve.

RECIPE TIP

Eat these tasty wraps with a homemade salsa or guacamole. You can find a recipe for each on pages 96 and 98.

AMARANTH TABOULI

INGREDIENTS

1 cup amaranth

1 cup rice milk or almond milk

1/2 green onion, diced

1 cup parsley, chopped

2 tablespoons fresh mint, chopped

1/2 cup lemon juice

1/4 cup extra virgin olive oil

2 cloves garlic, minced

2 tablespoons black & green olives, diced

HOW TO PREPARE

Simmer your amaranth in an equal volume of water for 10 minutes. Once cooked, allow amaranth to cool by placing it in your freezer for 15 minutes. Place all your ingredients except the olives in a bowl and mix together lightly. Place mix into freezer for 15 minutes to chill before serving. Garnish with your olives over top.

RECIPE TIP

Serve your tabouli over rye crackers for a creative way to enjoy this tasty and very healthy recipe.

Super Food

Amaranth Power

Amaranth is a super power food. For every grain that enters your mouth you are supplying your body with a large dose of high quality protein and complex carbohydrates as well as a large amount of calcium and iron. Amaranth is definitely a whole food to include into your diet as frequently as possible.

HOW TO USE

Amaranth cooks very quickly, making it an ideal choice for busy people. It only takes about ten minutes to prepare. Place equal amounts of amaranth and water in a saucepan and bring to boil. Once boiled, cover and simmer for 8 minutes.

SUGGESTIONS FOR DAILY USE

Breakfast: Add cooked amaranth to your cereal. You can even add a little to your favorite muffin or cookie recipe, or when baking homemade bread. I like to use it in my smoothies as well.

Lunch/Snack: Amaranth is great for a lunchtime boost. Just add a couple of cooked tablespoons to your salad or soups. You can even mix it with hemp seeds to create a nutritional power meal to fuel you for the rest of the day.

Dinner: The dinner options are endless with amaranth. Just add a few tablespoons to whatever you are eating. Amaranth can also be used as filler when preparing veggie burgers or over a stir-fry.

HOW TO STORE

Uncooked amaranth can be stored in a dark place in an airtight container. Once cooked, any leftover amaranth should be stored in the fridge. I tend to cook two cups of amaranth to take with me to work as a snack each week.

SHELF LIFE

Uncooked in the cupboard for 6 months; cooked in fridge for 5 days.

CORN & BLACK BEAN SALAD

INGREDIENTS

1 can organic black beans

1 can organic corn

1 cup cherry tomatoes, diced

1/4 cup of cilantro, chopped

4 tablespoons fresh lemon juice

1/4 cup extra virgin olive oil

1/2 small onion, diced

1 tablespoon prepared mustard

1/2 teaspoon Himalayan crystal salt

1/2 teaspoon fresh ground black pepper

HOW TO PREPARE

Drain the corn and beans and rinse with fresh water. Place all your ingredients into a large salad bowl mixing together gently and serve

RECIPE TIP

To spice it up a bit you can add 2 teaspoons of cayenne pepper. A little hit of heat goes very well with this salad and cayenne has a host of health benefits such as vitamin A.

Super Food

Black Bean Power

Black beans are low in fat and contain valuable minerals such as iron, calcium, potassium, magnesium and B vitamins. Black beans are also a great source of fiber and protein. Although they are not a complete protein, when added with grains or seeds, they form a high quality complete protein.

HOW TO USE

For canned beans, open and rinse with fresh water. For dried beans soak for 2 to 4 hours before cooking. This hydration helps to reduce cooking time. Strain water and place beans into a pot of fresh water and bring to a boil. Once boiled, reduce to a simmer until beans are soft, approx 45 minutes. Once done, strain, rinse and store in your fridge.

SUGGESTIONS FOR DAILY USE

Breakfast: Add some to your morning eggs. Why not try a little crushed black bean on toast with a little maple syrup?
Lunch/Snack: Add a handful to your soups, or toss some into your salad. You can even add them to your afternoon wrap.
Dinner: Black beans are a great thickener and provide a hearty texture to replace meat. Try them crushed up in a sauce or as your base for veggie burgers.

HOW TO STORE

Canned black beans will last for several years. Dried black beans should be stored in a dark place in an airtight container. Once cooked, black beans should be stored in the fridge. I tend to have two cans stocked for quick access throughout the week.

SHELF LIFE

Dried in cupboard for up to 6 months; cooked or opened in your fridge up to 4 days.

CUCUMBER & BASIL SALAD

INGREDIENTS

1 cucumber, chopped into little squares

2 tomatoes, diced into little squares

1/4 cup fresh basil, chopped

1/4 cup flax oil

2 tablespoons fresh lemon juice

1/2 teaspoon Himalayan crystal salt

1/2 teaspoon fresh ground black pepper

HOW TO PREPARE

Place all your ingredients together into a mixing bowl and toss.

RECIPE TIP

Garnish with some dried organic cranberries to sweeten the salad as well as adding some additional color to your plate.

SPRING QUINOA SALAD

INGREDIENTS

1 cup of quinoa

1 cup of sprouted sunflower seeds

1 red pepper, diced julienne style
(long skinny strips)

1/4 cup of organic raisins,
organic to avoid unwanted sulphites

1 tablespoon lemon juice

1/4 cup of sesame oil

2 tablespoons balsamic vinegar

1/2 teaspoon Himalayan crystal salt

1/2 teaspoon fresh ground black pepper

HOW TO PREPARE

Place your quinoa in a pot with two cups of water. Bring the water to a boil and let it simmer covered for 15 to 20 minutes. You want the quinoa a little mushy but not overcooked. Mix in all your other ingredients except the red pepper and sunflower sprouts. Place the quinoa in the refrigerator for 30 minutes. Once cooled, place your quinoa in a bowl and garnish with the red pepper and sprouts as desired.

RECIPE TIP

Make the same salad, but replace the quinoa with another nutritious grain such as amaranth or whole oat groats. This provides you more variety while including more whole grains into your diet.

QUINOA GREEK SALAD

INGREDIENTS

1 cup quinoa
1 tablespoon hemp seeds
1 tablespoon sunflower seeds
1/4 cup raisins
3/4 cup cherry tomatoes, sliced in half
1 cucumber, diced
1/2 red pepper, diced
1/4 cup black or green olives, diced
1/4 cup fresh basil, chopped
1 tablespoon lemon juice
1/4 cup organic goats cheese
1/2 red onion, diced
2 cloves garlic, minced
1/2 teaspoon Himalayan crystal salt
1/2 teaspoon fresh ground black pepper
3 tablespoons extra virgin olive oil
2 tablespoons balsamic vinegar

HOW TO PREPARE

Place your quinoa in a pot with 2 cup of water. Bring the water to a boil and let simmer covered for 15 to 20 minutes. You want the quinoa a little mushy but not over-cooked. Dice into small bite size pieces the tomatoes, cucumber, red pepper, onion and black or green olives. In a large mixing bowl place these ingredients and add fresh garlic, basil, salt and pepper. Now add the lemon juice, olive oil, balsamic vinegar, quinoa, hemp seeds, raisins and sunflower seeds and mix. Crumble the organic goats cheese over the top and serve.

RECIPE TIP

Try replacing the raisins with 1/2 cup of fresh local seasonal berries.

Super Food

Quinoa Power

Quinoa is a great source of fiber, complex carbohydrates, calcium, phosphorous, iron, vitamins B and E. If that wasn't enough, what makes quinoa so special is its protein content. Quinoa is one of the ideal ways to consume digestible protein. It is a complete protein, containing all the essential amino acids and is ideal for gluten intolerances.

HOW TO USE

Rinse your quinoa thoroughly by running it under fresh water. For every cup of quinoa, you will need 2 cups of water – cook it just as if you were cooking rice. Soak your quinoa and sprout it. You can watch a video of me sprouting my quinoa at www. PowerofFood.com.

SUGGESTIONS FOR DAILY USE

Breakfast: Sprinkle 2 cooked tablespoons into your morning cereal or smoothie or add on top of your morning toast.

Lunch/Snack: I take 6 tablespoons of cooked quinoa in a container on the road with me everyday and add it to just about anything I eat. This way I don't have to stress about eating healthy all the time, I just add the health without restrictions. Include some of the ground seeds into your container with the quinoa and you have a whole food mix you can use to increase the nutritional value of everything you eat. Just add a few tablespoons and away you go.

Dinner: Place 1/2 cup on a plate with vegetables of your choice and enjoy a very nourishing meal. Try adding some to stir-fries or on top of your pizza.

HOW TO STORE

Uncooked quinoa can be stored in a dark place in an airtight container. Cooked quinoa should be stored in your fridge.

SHELF LIFE

Uncooked in the cupboard for up to 6 months; cooked in fridge for 5 days.

SUNDRIED TOMATO & LENTIL SALAD

INGREDIENTS

2 cups spinach

1 can of organic lentils

3 tablespoons fresh rosemary, chopped

1/2 teaspoon Himalayan crystal salt

1/4 cup of sundried tomatoes, chopped

1/4 cup almonds, crushed

HOW TO PREPARE

If using canned lentils, just rinse with fresh water and place them in a large bowl. Soak your sundried tomatoes in a separate bowl with fresh water for 1 hour. Chop the tomatoes into small pieces and then combine all your ingredients (except the almonds) in a large salad bowl and mix. Garnish with the crushed almonds over top.

RECIPE TIP

Try any one of the amazing dressings shared with you in the *e3 for LIFE* recipe section to finish your salad off with style.

CREAMY DILL POTATO SALAD

INGREDIENTS

2 cups red potatoes

1/4 cup tahini

2 tablespoons fresh lemon juice

1 tablespoon fresh parsley

3 tablespoons fresh dill

2 tablespoons lemon zest

2 tablespoons prepared mustard

1/2 teaspoon Himalayan crystal salt

HOW TO PREPARE

Cut your potatoes into small quarter size. Steam them over medium heat for 20 minutes or till fork tender. Place steamed potatoes in your refrigerator to let cool for 20 minutes. Now add all your remaining ingredient and mix together gently.

RECIPE TIP

Add your choice of seeds or nuts to boost the flavor and nutritional value of every bite.

SUMMER AVOCADO SALAD

INGREDIENTS

1 avocado, cut into bite-sized pieces

1 mango, cut into bite-sized pieces

1/2 cup fresh blueberries

1 grapefruit, cut into bite-sized pieces

juice of 1/2 lime

2 tablespoons fresh mint, chopped

HOW TO PREPARE

Place all ingredients in a bowl or plate and spread mint over top.

RECIPE TIP

Add 3 tablespoons of hemp seeds and enjoy this salad as an early dinner option.

CRANBERRY KALE DELIGHT

INGREDIENTS

1 bunch of kale, chopped

1/2 cup dried cranberries

1/4 cup fresh lemon juice

HOW TO PREPARE

Chop your kale into small piece and place it in a large mixing bowl with the lemon juice. Squeeze the lemon juice into the kale. Be sure to really massage the lemon juice into the kale. The acid from the lemon juice will help break the kale down without using any heat, preserving its full nutritional value. Let the kale sit for 20 minutes in your refrigerator. Add cranberries over top and serve with any of your *e3 for LIFE* dressing recipes.

RECIPE TIP

Add some fresh local seasonal berries into the salad to replace the cranberries. So delicious and so healthy.

AVOCADO & CILANTRO SOUP

INGREDIENTS

1 avocado, chopped

1 cup fresh cilantro, chopped

2 tablespoons fresh lemon juice

1/2 teaspoon Himalayan crystal salt

1 cup fresh water

HOW TO PREPARE

Place all your ingredients into a blender or use a hand blender with all the ingredients in a pot with a flat bottom. Add more water as needed to reach your desired constancy.

RECIPE TIP

Add a little quinoa, hemp seeds or ground almonds to enhance the nutritional value of this amazing raw soup.

APPLE & BUTTERNUT SQUASH SOUP

INGREDIENTS

4 cups butternut squash, chopped

1 cup fresh apple juice

1 apple, diced

1 cup fresh water

1 teaspoon cinnamon

1/4 cup cashew, ground

1/2 teaspoon nutmeg

1/2 teaspoon Himalayan crystal salt

HOW TO PREPARE

Steam your squash gently for 15 minutes. Place all the ingredients into a blender and blend until smooth. That's it!

RECIPE TIP

Add 2 tablespoon of grated ginger for a little kick to your soup. Ginger has many health qualities when consumed raw such as decreasing inflammation and supporting your immune function.

HEART HEALTHY
LENTIL SOUP

INGREDIENTS

1 cup lentils

3 cups water

4 tablespoons fresh rosemary, chopped

1 onion, diced

4 cloves garlic, diced

1/2 teaspoon Himalayan crystal salt

1/2 teaspoon fresh ground black pepper

HOW TO PREPARE

Place all your ingredients into a medium saucepan and bring it to a boil. Once boiling, cover and reduce to simmer for 30 minutes. This is a great soup on a cold day to help warm your bones.

RECIPE TIP

Use a hand blender to purée your soup into a smoother texture. The smoother it is, the easier it is for digestion, which provides you with more energy.

PICK ME UP RAW SOUP

INGREDIENTS

2 large tomatoes

1 cucumber

1 avocado

3 handfuls of spinach

1-1/2 cups fresh water

1/4 cup of fresh dill

1/2 cup of cilantro

1 garlic clove

pinch of salt

2 pinches cayenne pepper

1 tablespoon flax oil

1 tablespoon hemp oil

HOW TO PREPARE

Blend all your ingredients in a food processor or blender until smooth. Drizzle with hemp or flax oil over top for added flavor and essential fatty acids.

RECIPE TIP

Add any combination of ground nuts or seeds to your soup to change the flavor, boost the nutritional value as well as alter the texture as you wish.

SPLIT PEA SOUP

INGREDIENTS

2-1/2 cups of split green peas

1 organic bouillon cube

5 cups fresh water

6 large carrots, diced

1/4 cup ginger, grated

1 large onion, diced

6 cloves of garlic, minced

1/2 teaspoon Himalayan crystal salt

1/2 teaspoon fresh ground black pepper

HOW TO PREPARE

Bring the water to a boil in a large pot and add all your ingredients. Simmer on low/medium heat with the lid over your pot for 30 minutes. Purée with a hand blender until you reach your desire constancy. Freeze any leftover soup to eat on another day.

RECIPE TIP

Increase the nutritional value by adding either quinoa, brown rice pasta or ground nuts of your choice to each bowl.

RAW CREAM OF CAULIFLOWER SOUP

INGREDIENTS

1/2 cauliflower, chopped

1/2 cup cashews, ground

2 tablespoons flax oil

2 tablespoons hemp oil

1 tablespoon lemon juice

1 cup fresh water

1/2 teaspoon nutmeg

1 tablespoon caraway seeds, ground

1/2 small onion, diced

1/2 teaspoon Himalayan crystal salt

1/2 teaspoon fresh ground pepper

HOW TO PREPARE

Soak your cashews in water for 30 minutes. Place all the ingredients into a blender or a food processor until desired constancy is reached. Garnish with crushed cashews.

RECIPE TIP

Add 2 soaked pitted dates into the blender to add a little sweetness. You can also try adding a 1/4 teaspoon of chipotle pepper to add a little heat.

Super Food

Green Pea Power

This legume offers an array of health benefits from good quality complex carbohydrates, a high amount of fiber, a great dose of protein, and a rich supply of iron as well as many other vitamins and minerals.

HOW TO USE

Split green peas do not need to be soaked before using and do not require hours of cooking to be enjoyed. If canned, just open and rinse. For dried peas, rinse 1 cup and add 4 cups of water to a pot. Bring to boil and then simmer over low heat until tender, about 30 minutes. Now your peas are ready to use in so many great recipes.

SUGGESTIONS FOR DAILY USE

Breakfast: Puree 1/2 cup of cooked split peas and add 2 teaspoons of hemp seed, ground sesame seed and ground flax seed to thicken into a paste. Spread over whole grain toast with a little natural honey.

Lunch/Snack: How about taking a little split pea soup to work – the recipe is now yours. Add a piece of whole grain bread or a couple of crackers and you have a powerful source of energy, sure to keep you going all day.

Dinner: Add cooked split peas into your pasta, or use in vegetable burgers or vegetable loaf recipes. Try adding them into stews or puree a cup and turn them into a tasty, nutritious sauce or dip.

HOW TO STORE

Canned green peas will last for several years. Dried green peas should be stored in a dark place in an airtight container. Once cooked, green peas should be stored in the fridge. I tend to have two cans stocked for quick access throughout the week.

SHELF LIFE

Dried in cupboard for 6 months; cooked or opened in your fridge for 4 days.

Super Food

Cashew Power

Cashews are a well rounded nut in that they offer you a balanced supply of essential fatty acids, fiber and quality protein. Cashews are also a good source of copper and iron. Plus cashews are also full of flavor.

HOW TO USE

Like almonds and pecans, cashews are also a great raw snack. Fresh cashews are an ideal food for a boost in your energy levels without receiving a big crash later. Cashews are available raw or as butter, milk and oil. Each option will provide you with a host of healthy benefits that should not be missed. I use cashews in any of my raw food recipes because of its ability to create smooth textures in certain recipes.

SUGGESTIONS FOR DAILY USE

Breakfast: Enjoy a morning boost with cashew milk. You can add whole, chopped or ground cashews into your morning cereal.
Lunch/Snack: Eat them raw. Add sliced cashews to your salad. Try spreading a little cashew butter on your sandwich. How about making a little extra morning smoothie to enjoy for lunch or snack?
Dinner: Add chopped cashews to your stir-fries and to any recipe for a nutritional and flavor boost. You can soak them overnight to turn them into a pâté or tasty spread just like almond or pecan.

HOW TO STORE

Due to the high content of essential fatty acids contained in cashews, it is important to store them in the fridge. Keep them stored in the door of your fridge for quick access, preferably next to all the other nuts, seeds and grains you now stock.

SHELF LIFE

Fridge for 3 months; freezer for 6 months.

CREAMY ZUCCHINI & SPINACH SOUP

INGREDIENTS

2 cups of zucchini, chopped

1-1/2 cup spinach

1 tablespoon lemon juice

1 tablespoon tahini

1/2 teaspoon Himalayan crystal salt

4 tablespoons fresh dill

1 cup fresh water

1 tablespoon flax oil

HOW TO PREPARE

Place all your ingredients into a blender and blend.

RECIPE TIP

Add a chopped avocado to increase the thickness and creaminess of the soup if desired.

RED PEPPER & HEMP SOUP

INGREDIENTS

2 large red peppers, chopped

1/2 cup hemp seeds

1/2 teaspoon Himalayan crystal salt

2 tablespoon fresh lemon juice

1/2 teaspoon curry powder

1/2 teaspoon cumin powder

1 teaspoon organic soy sauce

1 teaspoon fresh ground black pepper

1/2 cup fresh water

1/2 teaspoon caraway powder

HOW TO PREPARE

Place all your ingredients in a blender. Blend until smooth. Add more water as needed to reach desired constancy. Garnish with a few extra hemp seeds and fresh oregano.

RECIPE TIP

You may want to begin with 1/2 cup water and adjust based on the texture that you'd like as you go along!

Super Food

Hemp Power

Hemp seeds, also known as hemp hearts, are one of the world's most balanced and complete sources of food. If there is any one food to start including into your daily diet, this is the one. Hemp seeds are a complete source of protein, contain all the essential fatty acids and are an abundant source of vitamins, minerals and antioxidants. Hemp is also suitable for those unable to eat gluten, sugar, milk, nuts and meat.

HOW TO USE

Hemp seeds have a great nutty taste and are ideal when eaten raw. Unlike the flax seed, hemp does not need to be ground to receive all its nutritional value. Hemp is so easy to use. Add a tablespoon or two to the foods you like to eat. Hemp seeds are a great way to help control your blood sugar levels and avoid the mid-afternoon crashes. Next time you reach for that chocolate bar for a boost of energy, try some hemp seeds instead.

SUGGESTIONS FOR DAILY USE

Breakfast: Sprinkle 2 tablespoons into your cereal, smoothie or add a handful over top of your pancakes.

Lunch/Snack: Add 2 tablespoons of hemp seeds or hemp oil into soups or salads.

Dinner: Add a handful into stews, pasta dishes, over stir-fries, sprinkled over steamed vegetables – just add them to any meal without worry.

HOW TO STORE

Due to the high content of essential fatty acids contained in hemp seeds, it is important to store them in your fridge or freezer. Keep them stored in the door of your fridge for quick access.

SHELF LIFE

Fridge for 3 months; freezer for 6 months.

PISTACHIO MANGO SALSA

INGREDIENTS (MAKES 4 CUPS)

1/2 cup pistachios, chopped

1/2 red onion, diced

2 medium tomatoes, diced

1 mango, diced

2 cloves of garlic, minced

1/2 cup of fresh cilantro, chopped

1 avocado, cut into small pieces

1 tablespoon lemon juice

1/2 teaspoon Himalayan crystal salt

HOW TO PREPARE

Place all your ingredients into a medium-size bowl and gently mix together. Be careful not to mash up the avocado, they are delicate. Ready to serve.

RECIPE TIP

Try adding any number of seeds or nuts to the mix to create a variety of salsas for every occasion.

Super Food

Pistachio Power

Pistachios are a versatile and tasty nut. Not only do they provide a healthy dose of essential fatty acid, they also contain an ideal supply of iron and are known to help lower cholesterol – that is if you get them fresh, before they are roasted or salted. Pistachios are also a great source of protein and fiber. With this nut so high in vital nutrients, it should be a part of your daily diet.

HOW TO USE

Pistachios are great as a snack. You can also chop or grind pistachios to create any number of creative and delicious recipes. I often shell my fresh pistachios ahead of time and store them in the fridge so they are ready to add to recipes right away.

SUGGESTIONS FOR DAILY USE

Breakfast: Why not add some chopped pistachios into your pancake mix or add a little to your muffin mix? They are great just sprinkled in your morning smoothie or cereal.

Lunch/Snack: Eat them raw. Add chopped pistachios into your soup or salad. Try sprinkling ground pistachios on top of your sandwich. Add them to whatever you like to eat and feel a healthy boost in energy.

Dinner: Add chopped pistachios to any meal and enhance the flavor and nutritional power of every bite.

HOW TO STORE

Due to the high content of essential fatty acids contained in pistachios, it is important to store them in your fridge or freezer.

SHELF LIFE

Fridge for up to 3 months; freezer for 6 months.

GO TIME GUACAMOLE

INGREDIENTS (MAKES 2 CUPS)

2 avocado, chopped

1/2 red pepper, diced

4 cherry tomatoes, chopped

juice of 1 fresh lemon

juice of 1 fresh lime

1/4 cup extra virgin olive oil

1/2 onion, diced

3 cloves garlic, minced

1/2 cup fresh cilantro, chopped

1/2 teaspoon Himalayan crystal salt

1/2 teaspoon fresh ground peppers

HOW TO PREPARE

Using a fork, mash the avocado in a large bowl with the lemon and lime juice as well as salt and pepper. Be sure to leave the avocado a little chunky unless you prefer it very smooth. Now add the rest of your ingredients and mix together.

RECIPE TIP

Replace the olive oil with flax or hemp oil to increase the quality of essential fatty acids you consume. This recipe is also great with a little nuts or seeds added to create different varieties of guacamole.

OUTRAGEOUS OLIVE TAPENADE

INGREDIENTS (MAKES 1 CUP)

2 cloves garlic, minced

1 cup green olives, pitted and diced

1 cup black olives, pitted and diced

2 tablespoon capers

1 teaspoon fresh oregano, chopped

2 teaspoon fresh rosemary, chopped

1/4 cup fresh parsley, chopped

2 tablespoon fresh lemon juice

2 teaspoon freshly ground black pepper

3 tablespoon extra virgin olive oil

HOW TO PREPARE

Place all your ingredients (except the olive oil) into a food processor and blend together. Add the olive oil a little at a time to reach your desired consistency.

RECIPE TIP

Make extra because this recipe stores very well in an airtight container in your freezer to be used for a quick party snack.

CLASSIC ASIAN DRESSING

INGREDIENTS (MAKES 1 CUP)

1 teaspoon ginger, grated

3/4 cup extra virgin olive oil

2 tablespoons toasted sesame oil

juice of 1 fresh lime

2 teaspoons organic soy sauce

3 tablespoons pure natural maple syrup

HOW TO PREPARE

Blend all your ingredients in a blender until mixed.

RECIPE TIP

Add 1 cup of all natural peanut butter and serve as a tasty vegetable dip or use with spring rolls.

IN THE RAW RANCH DIP

INGREDIENTS (MAKES 1 CUPS)

1 cup cashews

1/4 cup extra virgin olive oil

1/2 teaspoon Himalayan crystal salt

1/4 cup fresh parsley

1 clove garlic, minced

1/4 cup fresh dill

1 tablespoon lemon juice

1 tablespoon flax oil

HOW TO PREPARE

Blend all your ingredients in a blender. Add more water as needed to reach desired constancy.

RECIPE TIP

Use this dip as an amazing dressing for any of the *e3 for LIFE* salad recipes or in a wrap or sandwich.

DREAMY AVOCADO DRESSING

INGREDIENTS (MAKES 1 CUP)

1 teaspoon cumin powder

2 tablespoons fresh lime juice

3 tablespoons flax oil, hemp or
    extra virgin olive oil

1 avocado

1/2 teaspoon Himalayan crystal salt

1 teaspoon prepared mustard

1 garlic clove, minced

1/4 cup fresh water

1 teaspoon fresh ground black pepper

HOW TO PREPARE

Place all your ingredients into a blender and blend. Add more water as needed to reach desired consistency.

RECIPE TIP

This is a great dressing to take to work and eat with fresh cut seasonal vegetables as an amazing snack.

SWEET SUNNY SUMMER DRESSING

INGREDIENTS (MAKES 1 CUP)

juice of 1/2 fresh lime

juice of 1/2 fresh lemon

juice of 1 fresh orange

1/2 teaspoon Himalayan crystal salt

1/2 cup fresh basil, chopped

1/2 cup extra virgin olive oil

1 tablespoon natural honey

HOW TO PREPARE

Put all your ingredients, except the oil, in a blender or food processor and blend on high until well combined. Next, with the motor running, add the oil in a thin stream, until the mixture is rich and emulsified.

RECIPE TIP

Add 2 teaspoons of grated ginger to add a little heat to this fresh and vibrant dressing.

ALMOND & HEMP SPREAD

INGREDIENTS (MAKES 2 CUPS)

1 cup almonds

2 teaspoons ginger, grated

1/2 teaspoon Himalayan crystal salt

2 tablespoons natural almond butter

juice of 1/2 fresh lemon

1/2 cup fresh water

1/2 cup hemp seeds

1/4 cup flax, hemp or extra virgin olive oil

HOW TO PREPARE

Soak your almonds for 24 hours. Once soaked discard the water and rinse your almonds. Place all your ingredients into a food processor except the hemp seeds. Once blended to a smooth paste, add your hemp seeds. Continue to blend adding more water as needed to reach your desired consistency.

RECIPE TIP

This dip is fantastic as a high energy, mid-afternoon snack or lunch option. Add a healthy scoop into your wraps, sandwiches or over whole grain crackers.

Super Food

Almond Power

High in protein, almonds are a great boost to the muscles and give you lasting energy through their high iron content. They are a great source of calcium, vitamin E and essential fatty acids. Almonds are sweet and make a great milk or butter kids enjoy.

HOW TO USE

Consume almonds that have been soaked for at least 12 to 24 hours to remove unwanted molds and to increase their digestibility. I tend to soak my almonds overnight and then place them into a dehydrator to regain their crunchiness. Raw almonds are an ideal food for relief from the mid-afternoon crashes and to avoid food cravings.

SUGGESTIONS FOR DAILY USE

Breakfast: Try a piece of sprouted grain bread with almond butter. How about a little almond milk with your smoothie or cereal, or add a handful to your cereal.

Lunch/Snack: Eat almonds raw and add them to your salad. Try spreading a little almond butter on a sandwich. How about making a little extra morning smoothie to enjoy for lunch or a snack?

Dinner: You can soak a cup of almonds overnight and turn them into a pâté or tasty spread. Rinse your cup of soaked almonds in the morning and place them into a food processor with a tablespoon of almond milk or water. Instant almond butter!

HOW TO STORE

Due to the high content of essential fatty acids contained in almonds, it is important to store your almonds in the fridge or freezer. Keep them stored in the door of your fridge for quick everyday access – next to all the other seeds you now stock.

SHELF LIFE

Fridge for 3 months, freezer for 6 months.

SUPER PESTO

INGREDIENTS (MAKES 2 CUPS)

2 cups basil, packed

1/4 teaspoon Himalayan crystal salt

2 tablespoons olive oil

1/4 cup pecans, crushed

1 tablespoon tahini

1 clove garlic

1/2 teaspoon lemon juice

HOW TO PREPARE

Blend all your ingredients in a food processor. You'll probably need to stop frequently to scrape down the bowl; you may need to add more oil, so use your judgment. Serve over a bowl of brown rice pasta or use as an amazing vegetable dip.

RECIPE TIP

Add 1/4 cup of your favorite crushed nut to boost the flavor and nutritional value of this pesto.

HEART WARMING THAI DRESSING

INGREDIENTS (MAKES 1 CUP)

1 avocado

1/4 cup cilantro, chopped

1 teaspoon cayenne powder

1 teaspoon ginger, grated

1/4 teaspoon Himalayan crystal salt

1/4 cup pitted dates, chopped

HOW TO PREPARE

Soak your dates for 20 minutes in 1 cup of water. Once soaked place all ingredient, including the water, into a blender and blend together. Add more water to reach your desired consistency.

RECIPE TIP

Add an extra avocado and enjoy this dressing as a dip with some fresh vegetables.

YES, I CAN STILL HAVE GRAVY

INGREDIENTS (MAKES 1 CUP)

1 can black beans

2 teaspoons organic soy sauce

1 teaspoon prepared mustard

1 teaspoon fresh ground black pepper

2 cloves garlic, minced

1/2 teaspoon Himalayan crystal salt

1/4 cup water

HOW TO PREPARE

Place all ingredients into a food processor and blend together. Add more water as needed to reach desired consistency. There is no need to heat this recipe, but feel free to do so if you want your gravy warmed.

RECIPE TIP

Pour this gravy over the top of my Sweet Potato Mash or Yummy Yam Fry recipes and enjoy without any feelings of guilt.

MAKE IT YOURSELF MAYO

INGREDIENTS (MAKES 1 CUP)

1 cup cashews

3 teaspoons fresh lemon juice

1/4 cup of flax, hemp or extra virgin olive oil

1 clove garlic, minced

1 tablespoon prepared mustard

1/4 cup of water

HOW TO PREPARE

Soak your cashews for 1 hour. Once soaked, remove the water and place all your ingredients into a food processor and blend together. Add more water as needed to reach your desired consistency.

RECIPE TIP

Try this mayo as a vegetable dip or on top of my veggie burger recipe.

BASIC VINAIGRETTE

INGREDIENTS (MAKES 1 CUP)

1/2 cup extra virgin olive oil

2 tablespoons fresh lemon juice

1 tablespoon prepared mustard

3 tablespoons balsamic vinaigrette

1/2 teaspoon Himalayan crystal salt

1/2 teaspoon fresh ground black pepper

HOW TO PREPARE

Using a whisk, mix all ingredients together and serve.

RECIPE TIP

Chop up a cup of kale. Place your kale in a bowl with 1/4 cup of this dressing. Massage the dressing into the kale. Leave your bowl in the refrigerator for 20 minutes and then serve.

CRUSHING CRANBERRY SAUCE

INGREDIENTS (MAKES 2 CUPS)

1 cup fresh apple juice

1 cup fresh orange juice

1 teaspoon cinnamon

1/2 teaspoon nutmeg

1/2 teaspoon allspice

1/2 cup pitted dates, chopped

1 cup cranberries, whole

1 cup pecans, chopped

1 cup dried cranberries

HOW TO PREPARE

Soak your dates for 20 minutes in the 1 cup of apple juice. Then place into a blender the apple juice, dates, spices and whole cranberries. Once your mixture reaches a smooth texture add the pecans and dried cranberries and blend further. Top with a few extra dried cranberries and chopped pecans.

RECIPE TIP

Place this sauce into a dehydrator for 24 hours and enjoy delicious fruit roll ups.

SNACKS

ZUCCHINI NUT MUFFINS

INGREDIENTS (MAKES 12 MUFFINS)

1 cup almond pulp –
   from making almond milk!

1/4 cup raw cane sugar

1/2 cup pitted dates

2 tablespoons hemp seeds

1/4 cup raisins

2 organic eggs

1 cup rice milk or almond milk

1/2 cup zucchini, shredded

1-1/2 cup brown rice flour

2 teaspoons baking powder

1/2 teaspoon baking soda

1/4 teaspoon pure vanilla extract

1/2 cup pecan, cashew, pistachio mix,
   chopped

HOW TO PREPARE

Soak your dates in 1/2 cup of water for 30 minutes then purée both in a blender. Combined all dry ingredients into one bowl and all wet ingredients into another bowl. Mix each bowl well. Add all wet ingredients into the bowl with your dry ingredients and mix together. Place the batter into a muffin pan and bake at 350°F for 30 minutes. Let cool and serve. You can freeze these muffins for a quick on the go snacks.

RECIPE TIP

The same batter makes an amazing cake, pancakes or cookies.

SWEET ROASTED PECANS

INGREDIENTS (MAKES 2 CUPS)

2 cups pecan halves

2 tablespoons butter

1/4 teaspoon Himalayan crystal salt

2 tablespoons raw cane sugar

HOW TO PREPARE

Spread your pecans on a baking pan and place the pan in the centre rack of your oven at 250°F. Mix occasionally, until they begin to brown, about 5 minutes. Once done, place the pecans into a bowl with the butter, sugar and salt. Mix all ingredients until each pecan has been coated. Return to the oven and roast for an additional 2 minutes.

RECIPE TIP

You can use this recipe as a snack or try adding them as a topping or garnish for other *e3 for LIFE* recipes. You can even add some hemp seeds to the mix before the final 2 minutes of baking.

Super Food

Pecan Power

Pecans are high in a number of essential nutrients. With an abundant amount of fiber in every bite, this nut is a must for increasing your energy levels throughout the day. With their natural maple flavor, pecans are a versatile addition to many of my recipes.

HOW TO USE

Just like almond, pecans are a great raw snack. Pecans can be consumed raw or as butter and milk. Each option will provide you with a host of healthy benefits that should not be missed. Since pecans have a high essential fatty acid content, it is important to store them properly in order to protect them from becoming rancid.

SUGGESTIONS FOR DAILY USE

Breakfast: Try adding pecan milk to your cereal. Grind a 1/4 cup of pecans in a coffee grinder into flour and place the flour into your morning cereal. Now add water instead of milk to enjoy amazing instant maple-like pecan milk that is so delicious.

Lunch/Snack: Eat them raw. Add sliced pecans into your salad. Try spreading a little pecan butter on your toast or make a little extra morning smoothie to enjoy for lunch or snack.

Dinner: Add chopped pecans to any recipe and taste the flavor boost. You can soak them overnight and then turn them into a pâté or tasty spread, like with almonds.

HOW TO STORE

Due to the high content of essential fatty acids contained in pecans, it is important to store them in your fridge or freezer. Keep them stored in the door of your fridge for quick access, preferably next to all the other nuts and seeds you now stock.

SHELF LIFE

Fridge for 3 months, freezer for 6 months.

HEAVENLY HALVAH

INGREDIENTS (MAKES 12 PIECES)

1/4 cup sesame seeds, ground

1/2 cup ground almonds

1/4 cup hemp seeds

4 tablespoons tahini

3 tablespoons natural honey

1/2 teaspoon Himalayan crystal salt

HOW TO PREPARE

Combine all your ingredients into a large mixing bowl. Mix until all the ingredients are combined together. Place the mixture into a square baking dish over wax or parchment paper. Sprinkle hemp seeds over top and place your halvah in your fridge for one hour. Once cooled, cut into small square portions and serve.

RECIPE TIP

How about adding in your favorite nuts or dried fruit? You can even add cocoa powder to make chocolate halvah.

Super Food

Sesame Power

S esame seeds are known for their health benefits. They have a great combination of carbohydrates, protein and fat. What makes this little seed so powerful is its high concentration of vitamins and minerals, especially magnesium, iron, calcium, zinc, copper and vitamin B.

HOW TO USE

Sesame seeds are great as is. They require no heating of any kind and can be added to increase nutritional value and flavor. Grind sesame seeds in a coffee grinder (not used for coffee) to release the essential oils and make them easier to digest. By doing so, you break the seed down, preparing it for your digestive system to use all those wonderful vitamins and minerals.

SUGGESTIONS FOR DAILY USE

Breakfast: Sprinkle 2 tablespoons of ground sesame seeds into your morning cereal or smoothie.

Lunch/Snack: Add 2 tablespoons of ground sesame seeds into your salad or soup. You can even add a handful of whole sesame seeds to your meal to add a nutty taste and a delicate, almost invisible, crunch to your meal.

Dinner: Just add some on top of whatever you are choosing to eat. YES, it's that simple to add the health!

HOW TO STORE

Due to the high content of essential fatty acids contained in sesame seeds, it is important to store them in your fridge or freezer. Keep them stored in the door of your fridge for quick access.

SHELF LIFE

Ground in fridge for up to 3 months; unground in freezer for up to 6 months.

MAGIC MACAROONS

INGREDIENTS (MAKES 14 MACAROONS)

3 cups unsulphured coconut

1/2 cup raw cane sugar

4 organic egg whites

1/4 teaspoon Himalayan crystal salt

1/2 teaspoon pure vanilla extract

1/2 teaspoon cinnamon

HOW TO PREPARE

In a large mixing bowl mix until combined the coconut, raw cane sugar, salt, egg whites, cinnamon, and vanilla extract. Pack mix into small teaspoon-size balls and place them on a baking sheet. Bake at 350°F for 15 minutes or until golden brown. So easy!

RECIPE TIP

Try adding 1/3 cup cocoa powder to make chocolate macaroons.

POWER DATE BARS

INGREDIENTS (MAKES 10 BARS)

1/4 cup flax seeds, ground

1/4 cup sesame, ground

1/4 cup sunflower, ground

1/4 cup hemp seeds

1/4 cup shredded coconut

2 cups pitted dates, chopped

2 tablespoons water

HOW TO PREPARE

Place dates into a food processor with water and blend. Add all the other ingredients and blend together. Cover a square baking dish with wax or parchment paper and place mixture evenly about 1 inch thick to be cut into bars when done. Refrigerate overnight. Cut into bar serving sizes and freeze to be eaten when desired.

SPECIAL WEBSITE FEATURE

Visit **www.PowerofFood.com** and sign up for my monthly Ezine to instantly receive a video on how to prepare my amazing energy bars.

RECIPE TIP

Try making these bars with other dried fruit such as raisins, apricots or cranberries.

Super Food

Coconut Power

Power Date Bars *Page 112*

Though its name suggests that it is a nut, I've always regarded coconut as a fruit, but it is actually a seed. When the coconut is young, it has properties like fruit, and as it matures, it becomes nuttier. Coconut contains fiber, iron and protein and is one of the only sources of saturated fat that is healthy for you to consume.

HOW TO USE

Coconut is great raw. Use coconut shredded; the oil of the coconut is a great addition to any raw or low heat recipe as coconut meal; and the milk of the coconut such as what is found in curry or Thai dishes.

SUGGESTIONS FOR DAILY USE

Breakfast: Sprinkle 2 tablespoons of shredded, unsulphured coconut into your cereal, smoothie or baked goods such as muffins or breads.

Lunch/Snack: Try a little coconut oil in your salad dressing or soups.

Dinner: Coconut milk is ideal in many recipes such as Thai curries and coconut soups or added to a dip.

HOW TO STORE

Store your dried coconut in a cool, dry place.

SHELF LIFE

If you buy your shredded coconut fresh, it will last for several months in the cupboard. You can also freeze it to extend the shelf life to 6 months.

HIGH ENERGY TRAIL MIX

INGREDIENTS (MAKES 3 CUPS)

1/2 cup of cacao nips

1/2 cup dried cherries, cranberries, raisins or
blueberries

1/2 cup raw almond

1/2 cup raw walnuts

1/2 cup raw sunflower seeds

1/2 cup of pumpkin seeds

HOW TO PREPARE

Place all ingredients into a storage container and mix. Now all you need to do is grab a handful to help control your blood sugar when you get your next food craving.

RECIPE TIP

Get creative. Add any number of dried fruits, nuts and seeds to the mix to create different variations. I take a bag of my trail mix on the road with me everywhere I go.

KALE CHIPS

INGREDIENTS (MAKES 1 LARGE BAG)

1 bunch of kale

2 tablespoons lemon juice

1 tablespoon stone ground mustard

1 tablespoon ground black pepper

1 tablespoon grated ginger

1/4 cup organic soy sauce

HOW TO PREPARE

Chop your kale into chip size pieces. Place all the ingredients (without kale) into a bowl and mix. Now add the kale and mix well. Place the kale onto your dehydrator tray and dehydrate for 12 hours. If you do not have a dehydrator, you can lay the kale out on a baking sheet and bake at 115°F for two hours with the lip of the oven open.

SPECIAL WEBSITE FEATURE

Visit **www.PowerofFood.com** to watch a video on how to prepare this great recipe.

RECIPE TIP

Double this recipe to ensure you have plenty of chips on hand. The more you make, the easier it is to avoid buying commercial potato chips.

AWESOME DRIED MANGO

INGREDIENTS (MAKES 2 CUPS)

1 mango

HOW TO PREPARE

Peel the skin off the mango. Slice your mango into thin pieces and place them onto your dehydrator trays. Dehydrate for 24 hours. Store in an airtight container.

SPECIAL WEBSITE FEATURE

Visit **www.PowerofFood.com** to watch a video on how to prepare this amazing recipe

RECIPE TIP

Take this yummy treat when on the road for a healthy snack and a quick boost of energy.

YUMMY YUMMY
YAM FRIES

INGREDIENTS (MAKES 1 LARGE BOWL)

2 large yams, peeled

1 teaspoon Himalayan crystal salt

1 tablespoon fresh ground black pepper

4 tablespoons extra virgin olive oil

HOW TO PREPARE

Preheat your oven to 350°F. Slice your yams into thin French fry pieces. In a large mixing bowl place salt, pepper and oil and mix together. Now add the yams and mix until all yams are well coated. Add more oil if needed. Place the yams on a baking tray and bake for 30 minutes or until a little golden brown. Yum Yum Yam Fries!

RECIPE TIP

Add 2 tablespoons of cayenne pepper into the oil mix to spice up your yam fries.

LENTIL SHEPHERD PIE

INGREDIENTS (MAKES 6 SLICES)

1 can organic black beans

2 cans organic lentils

6 medium potatoes, diced

1 organic egg

1/2 cup rice milk or almond milk

2 tablespoons organic butter

1 teaspoon Himalayan crystal salt

1 teaspoon fresh ground black pepper

1 cup carrots, chopped

1 cup broccoli, chopped

1 medium onion, diced

4 cloves garlic, minced

1 tablespoon prepared mustard

2 tablespoons fresh basil

2 tablespoons rosemary

HOW TO PREPARE

Boil potatoes until tender, place into a food processor and blend together with milk and butter. Set aside. Now sauté the onions and garlic with a little olive oil for 2 minutes. In a food processor combine all remaining ingredients except the potatoes.

Blend the ingredients together lightly to ensure the mix remains chunky. Place the mix into a medium size baking dish, spread your mashed potatoes over top and bake at 350°F for 30 to 35 minutes.

RECIPE TIP

Garnish with a healthy serving of ground nuts or seeds over top to increase the flavor and nutritional value of every bite.

Super Food

Lentil Power

Lentils are another super food that are often overlooked. This legume has a high amount of complex carbohydrates and offers an abundant supply of iron. Eating lentils will ensure you receive a boost to your energy levels and avoid unwanted fatigue.

HOW TO USE

Lentils, like split green peas, do not need to be soaked before using and do not require hours of cooking to be enjoyed. If canned, just open and rinse. For dried lentils, rinse 1 cup and add 4 cups of water to a pot. Bring to boil and then simmer over low heat until tender, about 30 minutes. Now your lentils are ready to use in so many great recipes.

SUGGESTIONS FOR DAILY USE

Breakfast: Purée 1/2 cup of cooked lentils and add 2 teaspoons of hemp seed, ground sesame seed and ground flax seed to thicken into a paste. Spread over whole grain toast with a little natural honey and enjoy.

Lunch/Snack: How about taking some cooked lentils to work to add to your soup or salad? How much work would it be to have a can of lentils to open at work? This is one powerful helping of energy, sure to keep you going all day.

Dinner: Add cooked lentils into any vegetable recipe such as burgers or vegetable loaf recipes. Try adding them into your stews or purée a cup and turn them into a tasty, nutritious sauce or dip.

HOW TO

Canned lentils will last for several years. Dried lentils should be stored in a dark place in an airtight container. Once cooked, lentils should be stored in the fridge. I tend to have two cans stocked for quick access throughout the week.

SHELF LIFE

Dried in cupboard for 6 months, cooked or opened in your fridge for 4 days.

EASY GRAIN RISOTTO

INGREDIENTS (MAKES 4 CUPS)

2 cups quinoa

2 cups rice milk or almond milk

2 tablespoons butter

1 teaspoon Himalayan crystal salt

1 teaspoon fresh ground black pepper

1 medium onion, diced

2 cloves garlic, minced

1 organic vegetable bouillon cube

2 tablespoons fresh herbs, chopped

HOW TO PREPARE

In a medium saucepan cook the onion and garlic in butter over medium heat for 2 minutes. Now add the quinoa. Cook and stir for 2 more minutes. Stir in the water, bouillon cube, salt and pepper. Bring to a boil and reduce heat to simmer. Simmer, covered, for 15-20 minutes. The mixture when done should be a little creamy. If necessary, add in a little more milk to reach your desired consistency. For the final touch garnish with a tablespoon of hemp seeds.

RECIPE TIP

Make double the amount to have a little lunch tomorrow. Try using amaranth or millet to create a different style risotto.

ULTIMATE VEGGIE BURGERS

INGREDIENTS (MAKES 8 BURGERS)

2 cans organic black beans

1 organic egg

2 teaspoons lemon juice

5 slices sprouted grain bread

1 teaspoon Himalayan crystal salt

1 teaspoon fresh ground black pepper

2 cups vegetables of choice, chopped

1 medium onion, diced

4 cloves garlic, minced

1 tablespoon prepared mustard

2 tablespoons of your favorite spices

2 tablespoons of your favorite herbs

HOW TO PREPARE

Toast the bread and place it into a food processor to make breadcrumbs and set aside.

Sauté the onions and garlic with a little olive oil for 2 minutes. In a large mixing bowl combine all your ingredients but not the bread. Place the mix into the food processor. In a separate bowl add the blended mix in with the breadcrumbs. Make into patty size portions and bake at 350°F for 35 minutes or barbecue if you like. If your mixture is too moist, try adding another cup of toasted breadcrumbs.

RECIPE TIP

Add 1/4 cup of any ground nuts or seeds to the mix before baking to enhance the nutritional value and taste of each burger.

BROWN RICE LOAF

INGREDIENTS (MAKES 6 SLICES)

1/2 cup sesame seeds

1/2 cup sesame seeds, ground

1 organic egg

1/2 cup organic ketchup

1 red pepper, diced

1 cup long grain brown rice

1 small onion, diced

2 gloves garlic

1 teaspoon fresh ground black pepper

1 teaspoon Himalayan crystal salt

1/2 cup extra virgin olive oil

4 tablespoon oregano & basil, chopped

HOW TO PREPARE

Make your rice and set it aside. In a food processor, combine the red pepper, onion, garlic, black pepper, egg and olive oil. Blend until smooth. In a large mixing bowl combine the mix with your sesame seeds and rice and mix together. Put your mix into a loaf-style baking pan. Bake at 350°F for 45 minutes.

RECIPE TIP

Add a 1/4 cup of hemp seeds and ground flax seeds to increase the nutritional punch. Why not double the portion size and make two loafs, one for tonight and freeze the other to enjoy when you need a quick lunch or dinner? Top it of with my *Yes, I Can Still Eat Gravy* recipe for the perfect combo.

Super Food

Brown Rice Power

Brown Rice is a great alternative to popular gluten-based grains. As a gluten-free grain, brown rice is also an amazing source of complex carbohydrates as well as quality protein and several vitamins and minerals.

HOW TO USE

Place brown rice in a sauce pan in a two-to-one ratio of water to rice. Bring to a boil and let simmer until tender (approx 30 to 40 minutes). Stir occasionally. Add a teaspoon of extra virgin olive oil and dash of Himalayan crystal salt once boiling. Be sure to keep an eye on the rice to ensure you do not burn it. I tend to cook a little extra to have for lunch the next day.

SUGGESTIONS FOR DAILY USE

Breakfast: Cook as above and add a little maple syrup, unsulphured raisins and enjoy as a healthy breakfast boost.

Lunch/Snack: Add a handful of cooked brown rice to your salad or soup. You can even find at your grocery store brown rice wraps to use as an alternative to wheat-based wraps.

Dinner: Use brown rice as a nutritional side dish for any number of tasty meals.

HOW TO STORE

Uncooked brown rice should be stored in a dark place in an airtight container. Once cooked, brown rice should be stored in the fridge. I tend to cook two cups of brown rice each week and store in my fridge for quick, daily access.

SHELF LIFE

Uncooked in cupboard for 6 months; cooked in fridge for 5 days.

STUFFED BUTTERNUT SQUASH

INGREDIENTS (MAKES 2 HALVES)

1 tablespoon each of flax, hemp &
   sesame seeds

1/4 cup cranberries

juice of 1/2 a fresh lemon

1 teaspoon mustard

1 butternut squash

1/4 cup extra virgin olive oil

2 tablespoons basil, chopped

1/2 cup sunflower seeds

1/4 cup sunflower seeds, ground

HOW TO PREPARE

Cut the squash in half and remove the seeds. With a fork, make small holes throughout the entire inside. In a small mixing bowl place the lemon juice, olive oil, basil and mustard then pour into the holes. Bake the squash face up for 45 minutes at 350°F. or until a fork pushes through easily. Place the seeds and cranberries on top and serve.

RECIPE TIP

Include a cup of brown rice or quinoa to increase the nutritional value of the stuffing.

Super Food

Sunflower Power

Sunflowers are a great source of protein, fiber and carbohydrates, but what makes this seed so powerful is its healthy dose of essential fatty acids and Vitamin E as well as a great mix of B vitamins.

HOW TO USE

Sunflower seeds are great raw as a snack or in any recipe. Like most seeds there is no heating required and they can be added to increase the nutritional value and flavor of any recipe.

SUGGESTIONS FOR DAILY USE

Breakfast: Sprinkle 2 tablespoons into your eggs, cereal or smoothie.

Lunch/Snack: Grind 2 tablespoons in a coffee grinder and spread on your sandwich, wrap or put into your soup or salad.

Dinner: Grind some sunflower seeds and add them into your mashed potatoes or mixed in with a little wild rice.

HOW TO STORE

Due to the high content of essential fatty acids contained in sunflower seeds, it is important to store them in your fridge or freezer. Keep them stored in the door of your fridge for quick access.

SHELF LIFE

In the fridge for 3 months; in the freezer for 6 months.

PUMPKIN SEED PÂTÉ IN CHARD

INGREDIENTS (MAKES 8 WRAPS)

1-1/4 cup pumpkin seeds

juice from 1 fresh lemon

1/4 cup flax or hemp oil

4 tablespoons fresh parsley, chopped

1/2 teaspoon ginger, grated

8 green chard leaves, to wrap pâté in.

2 garlic cloves, minced

1/2 onion, diced

1 teaspoon cayenne powder

1 teaspoon natural honey

1/2 teaspoon fresh ground black pepper

1/2 teaspoon Himalayan crystal salt

HOW TO PREPARE

Soak your pumpkin seeds in fresh water overnight. Place the soaked seeds (rinsed and strain) in a food processor with the rest of the ingredients. Once puréed, place a small scoop into a piece of fresh chard and wrap. Now that's a healthy and delicious meal to impress.

RECIPE TIP

Try adding a little prepared mustard to the mix to change up the flavor if desired.

Super Food

Pumpkin Power

Pumpkin seeds are a great source of protein, fiber and carbohydrates, but what makes it so powerful is its healthy dose of Vitamin E as well as a great mix of B vitamins.

HOW TO USE

Pumpkin seeds are a great raw snack or in any recipe. Like most seeds there is no heating required and they can be added to increase the nutritional value and flavor of any recipe.

SUGGESTIONS FOR DAILY USE

Breakfast: Sprinkle 2 tablespoons into your eggs, cereal or smoothie. You can even add some on top of your morning bagel or toast.

Lunch/Snack: Grind 2 tablespoons in a coffee grinder and spread on your warp or sandwich. Add a few to your soup or salad.

Dinner: Grind some pumpkin seeds and add 2 tablespoons into your mashed potatoes or mixed in with your chili or stew.

HOW TO STORE

Due to the high content of essential fatty acids contained in pumpkin seeds, it is important to store them in your fridge. Keep them stored in the door of your fridge for quick access.

SHELF LIFE

Fridge for 3 months; freezer for 6 months.

COCONUT QUINOA CURRY

INGREDIENTS (MAKES 6 BOWLS)

1 can coconut milk

1 cup quinoa

1 large onion diced

4 cloves garlic chopped

2 tablespoon curry powder

2 tablespoon cilantro, basil &
    rosemary chopped

1 can organic corn

3 potatoes, diced

3 sweet potatoes, diced

3 cups fresh water

juice of 1/2 fresh lemon

1 large tomato diced

1 tablespoon prepared mustard

2 tablespoons ginger, grated

1/2 zucchini, diced

1/2 broccoli, diced

1 cup spinach

1 mango

1/2 teaspoon fresh ground black pepper

1/2 teaspoon Himalayan crystal salt

HOW TO PREPARE

Cook your potatoes for 15 minutes in boiling water. Simmer your quinoa for 15 minutes in a separate pot. Place all other ingredients into a large pot and simmer for 20 minutes. Add the cooked quinoa and potatoes to the large pot and let simmer for an additional 10 minutes.

RECIPE TIP

Garnish each bowl with some freshly ground cashews for extra flavor and a nutritional boost.

SPECIAL WEBSITE FEATURE

Visit **www.PowerofFood.com** to watch a video on how to prepare this amazing recipe.

BROWN RICE TORTILLA PIZZA

INGREDIENTS (MAKES 2 PIZZAS)

2 brown rice tortillas

5 tablespoons extra virgin olive oil

4 cloves garlic, minced

2 medium tomatoes, diced

1 red pepper, diced

1 onion, diced

1 teaspoon fresh rosemary

1 teaspoon fresh basil

1 cup organic cheese of choice, shredded

HOW TO PREPARE

Preheat your oven to 350°F. Brush each tortilla with 1 tablespoon of olive oil. In a large mixing bowl, mix all your ingredients (except the cheese) with 3 tablespoons of olive oil. Place the ingredients evenly throughout each tortilla. Top each piece with your shredded cheese. Bake pizzas for about 10 minutes or until the cheese is melted.

RECIPE TIP

Use my *Hungry Hungry Hummus* recipe as a sauce for this pizza. You will enjoy it!

SWEET POTATO & TURNIP MASH

INGREDIENTS (MAKES 4 CUPS)

5 sweet potatoes, peeled and chopped

3 large turnips, peeled and chopped

2 tablespoons prepared mustard

2 tablespoons flax oil

1/4 cup of rice milk or almond milk

1 tablespoon natural honey

1/2 teaspoon nutmeg

1/2 teaspoon Himalayan crystal salt

1/2 teaspoon fresh ground peppers

HOW TO PREPARE

Steam your potatoes and turnips for 20 minutes or until very tender. Place your ingredients into a food processor and blend until smooth.

RECIPE TIP

Serve your mash in a wine glass at your next party with my *Yes, I Can Still Eat Gravy* recipe spread over top. You will be a crowd favorite.

MUSHROOM ALMOND STUFFING

INGREDIENTS (MAKES 4 CUPS)

2 portobello mushrooms, chopped

1/4 cup olive oil

1/4 cup organic soy sauce

1 tablespoon apple cider vinegar

3 cups almonds

2 teaspoons fresh oregano, chopped

2 teaspoons fresh rosemary, chopped

2 teaspoons fresh parsley, chopped

1/2 cup carrots, chopped

1/2 cup celery, chopped

HOW TO PREPARE

Marinade the chopped mushrooms in the olive oil, organic soy sauce and apple cider vinegar and place overnight in your fridge. When ready, blend the mushrooms in a food processor with the almonds and fresh herbs. Now place the carrots and celery into the blender and mix. Add extra virgin olive oil or flax oil to the mixture to reach your desired consistency.

RECIPE TIP

Add some dried raisins or cranberries to give it a little sweetness to your stuffing.

ULTIMATE RAW CHOCOLATE MOUSSE

INGREDIENTS (MAKES 2 CUPS)

1 cup cashews

1 tablespoon natural honey

1/2 teaspoon vanilla

4 tablespoons all natural cocoa powder

1/2 cup + 1 tablespoon fresh water

HOW TO PREPARE

Soak your cashews for 1 hour. Once soaked, discard the water and place all the ingredients in a food processor and blend. Add more water to reach your desire consistency.

RECIPE TIP

Top with seasonal fresh berries. You can also add 1 tablespoon of hemp seeds or 1 tablespoon of ground almonds to each serving to boost the flavor and nutritional value of every bite.

FLOURLESS HEMP PEANUT BUTTER COOKIES

INGREDIENTS (MAKES 8 COOKIES)

1 cup of hemp seeds

1/4 cup raw cane sugar

2 organic eggs

1 cup all natural peanut butter

1/2 teaspoon baking soda

1/4 cup organic chocolate chips

HOW TO PREPARE

Mix together all your ingredients in a large bowl. Spoon out small ball-size portions and flatten onto parchment paper with a fork. Cook in your oven at 350°F until golden brown, 10 to 15 minutes. So tasty and so nutritious, kids love them!

RECIPE TIP

Add 1/2 teaspoon each of cinnamon, nutmeg, allspice and all-natural vanilla extract to add variety and flavor to your cookies.

PECAN CHOCOLATE SPICE COOKIES

INGREDIENTS (MAKES 8 COOKIES)

1-1/2 cups pecans

1 cup pitted dates, chopped

1/4 cup hemp seeds

1/2 cup shredded dried coconut

2 tablespoons all natural cocoa powder

1/2 teaspoon Himalayan crystal salt

1/2 teaspoon grated ginger

1 teaspoon cinnamon

1/2 teaspoon nutmeg

1/2 teaspoon vanilla extract

2 tablespoons fresh water

HOW TO PREPARE

Soak your pecans in water for 1 hour. Blend all your ingredients in a food processor until the mixture begins to stick together when pressed between your fingers. On a cutting board place individual cookie-sized portions. Press down into desired shape and serve. That's it!

RECIPE TIP

Try replacing the pecans for a different nut to make several varieties.

I CAN'T BELIEVE IT'S APPLE PIE

INGREDIENTS (MAKES 1 MEDIUM PIE)

1/2 cup pecans

1/2 cup almonds

1/2 cup pitted dates, chopped

2 apples, chopped in food processor

1/2 teaspoon cinnamon

1/2 teaspoon nutmeg

1/2 teaspoon allspice

2 teaspoon fresh lemon juice

HOW TO PREPARE

Place the pecans, almonds and dates into a food processor. Once blended together, spread the mixture into a pie plate evenly to serve as the crust. Take 1 apple and place it into your food processor and blend it with all the other ingredients. Place the filling into a bowl and add the second apple, diced into small pieces. Spread the mix over the crust. Add more apples as desired. Garnish with 1/2 cup of chopped pecans.

RECIPE TIP

Replace the apples for any other fruit and voilà, instant pie with endless varieties.

CHOCOLATE POPCORN

INGREDIENTS (MAKES 1 LARGE
PARTY BOWL)

1 cup organic kernels of corn

1 tablespoon extra virgin olive oil

1 teaspoon Himalayan crystal salt

1/2 cup organic chocolate chips

2 tablespoons of rice milk or almond milk

HOW TO PREPARE

Place the corn in a pot over medium heat
with the olive oil and cover. Shake the pot
hovering close to the element, but not right
on top of it. Keeping the steam held inside
is the key to making great popcorn. Within
5 minutes the corn will begin to pop. Keep
shaking until all kernels are popped. Do
not open the pot or you lose all the steam
and no more popping. In a sauce pan place
chocolate chips and milk over medium heat
until melted. Pour over your popcorn and
mix until coated. Place the popcorn in your
freezer for 1 hour to harden the chocolate.

RECIPE TIP

Enhance the nutritional value by mixing
hemp seeds in with the chocolate before
coating your popcorn.

Super Food

Corn Power

My wife is from Québec, Canada. I grew up eating a lot of corn on the cob being from Ontario, but the Québeçois, they know how to eat corn. At some sittings I have seen my friends and family each eat up to 6 cobs. Corn, when grown organic, is a healthy source of fiber, B vitamins, vitamin C as well as phosphorus. The biggest difference between organic popcorn kernels versus "traditional" popcorn kernels is air... and taste. Regular popcorn has a very high expansion ratio, which means that popped kernels are mostly air. This translates to less flavor. Many organic farmers choose to grow varieties with lower ratios, which means they have a more robust corn flavor.

HOW TO USE

Popcorn is an excellent food for snacking because it is easy to prepare and you can have a decent portion size. You can either use a hot air popper or you can prepare in a pot on the stove. There are also many different ways in which you can dress the popcorn for variety and flavor.

SUGGESTIONS FOR DAILY USE

Snack: Prepare popcorn ahead of time and pack it as part of your lunch as a snack. In addition you can eat popcorn as a snack anytime during the day. Remember to introduce different flavors to make it exciting. Perhaps introduce your favorite organic spices or a little nutritional yeast or butter.

HOW TO STORE

Uncooked corn can be stored in a dark place in an airtight container. Once popped, popcorn should be stored in a cool dry location.

SHELF LIFE

Cupboard for 6 months; popped in cupboard for 7 to 10 days depending on what you used to flavor it.

THAT'S AN AMAZING RAW STRAWBERRY CHEESECAKE

INGREDIENTS (MAKES ONE LARGE CAKE)

2 cups cashews

2 cups pitted dates, chopped

2 tablespoons pure maple syrup

1/2 teaspoon Himalayan crystal salt

1 cup almonds

1 cup fresh organic strawberries

1/2 cup water

2 tablespoons natural cocoa powder

HOW TO PREPARE

Crust: Soak your dates in water for 1 hour (keep the water). Soak your cashews in water for 1 hour and then discard the water. Grind your almonds in a coffee grinder (not used for coffee). Remove the dates from the water, but keep the water aside for later. Place your dates into a food processor with the cocoa powder and blend together. Add a little of the date water as you blend to be sure to create a paste. You don't want it too moist. In a mixing bowl place your date paste and mix in your ground almonds until batter is formed. Spread the batter into a pie dish.

Topping: In a blender, place your soaked cashews, no water, and blend. Add into the blender 1/4 cup of the date water, maple syrup, strawberries and salt. Blend until smooth. Add more date water to reach a smooth texture, but not too runny. Place mixture over top of piecrust and top with extra strawberries and almonds. Place the pie in your refrigerator for 2 hours and serve.

RECIPE TIP

You can make any variety of cheesecake just by changing the fruit you add, such as banana, apple, peach or blueberry. It's your choice. You can even change the crust by replacing the almonds with pecans or another of your favorite nut or seed.

RAW RAW BROWNIES

INGREDIENTS (MAKES 6 BROWNIES)

1/2 cup almond butter

2 cups pitted dates, chopped

3 tablespoons natural cocoa powder

2 tablespoons water

HOW TO PREPARE

Place your dates into a food processor with the water and blend together. Add all your other ingredients and blend together. Cover a square baking dish with wax or parchment paper and place mixture evenly throughout. You want the mix to be about 1 inch thick to be cut into small brownie sizes. Refrigerate overnight. Cut your mixture into small brownie serving sizes and freeze them to be eaten when you desired.

RECIPE TIP

Roll the finished mixture into little balls. On a separate plate, place 1/2 cup hemp seeds or coconut or cocoa powder. Now roll each ball over top until coated. You now have amazing truffles to impress at your next party.

Get Creative

Each of the recipes I designed to be easy for you to bring healthier whole, plant-based foods into your life. The more you try the different recipes, the quicker you will experience success reaching your desired results. I promise you, if you make the effort and get creative with whole foods, you will reach the ideal 80% of the 80/20 Rule with ease and without any restrictions to your diet or lifestyle. How's that for a promise?

I have now shared with you the first element of *e3 for LIFE*, FOOD. Now it is time to introduce you to element number 2, THOUGHTS. When you begin to eat more nutritious foods in combination with healthier thoughts, it is unbelievable what you can accomplish in every area of your life. Do you want it bad enough? If you do, read on.

PART 3

THOUGHTS

THE POWER OF YOUR MIND

What is the most powerful part of your body? If you said your brain, you would be correct. At only 3 pounds, your brain is the processing centre for every thought you have and it is your thoughts that produce every result you currently experience. If you would have told me I would be talking about the power of your thoughts back when I was sick and unhealthy, I would have said you are "nuts". I am so happy to share with you this valuable information below. In combination with eating healthier, engaging my thoughts in a more positive way unleashed a universal power I never knew existed. If you are willing to be open to what you are about to read, your results will come quickly, easily and last a lifetime, I PROMISE.

THE FAILING SYSTEM

Earlier I touched on the fact that we are what I call a "2nd generation fast food eater" society. During this discussion it was revealed that we have become a society disconnected from our relationship to food. This disconnect has led many of us down a very unhealthy road. Even further impacting our health has been our over-dependency on having everything quick and easy, from food to technology and even more damaging, our health as well.

We have become a result driven society of people who want everything on demand, including our health. Is that realistic?

We spend thousands of dollars on diets, supplements, cleanses and prescriptions drugs. The health care industry is a multi-billion dollar a year business yet it is dominated by one-dimensional solutions. What is a one-dimensional solution? Any solution that does not get to the root cause of why we take the action we take. It is in our daily actions that we produce our results. Without getting to the roots of our actions, you will undoubtedly keep experiencing the same results over and over again. Every single result you currently experience begins with a single thought.

What happens when you are not successful on your latest diet? I know what I went thought in the past. Feelings of anger, frustration and guilt dominated my mind when I failed to finish a diet or maintain my results. Do you remember how you felt during your last attempt at losing weight or striving to accomplish a health goal? Our demand for one-dimensional solutions has over saturated the North American market with options that lead many of us to experiencing failure over and over again. When you experiencing failure, how do you feel?

On average we have about 60,000 thoughts per day. Each thought you have produces a feeling that you experience. It is your feelings that lead to every action you take.

What do you call an action that you take over and over again?

It is called a habit. So if your thoughts produce your feelings and your feelings produce your actions, your habits are a direct result of your dominant thoughts.

What are your dominant thoughts made up of? Are they positive or negative? All you need to do is take a look at every result you currently have and you will find your answer.

The sequence of your thoughts determining your results finds its explanation in basic quantum physics. We are all made up of energy and everything moves in frequencies, even your thoughts. If you send out a negative thought, your thought emits a frequency (sometimes called a 'vibration') of energy that acts like a magnet, attracting back into your energy field a negative-vibration result. If you want to change your results to something positive, you need to emit a positive frequency or vibration.

WE ARE ALL ENERGY

Energy is in everything and we are all made up of it. Without internalizing and accepting this basic concept you will forever battle with your health as well as all your life results. If we are all made up of energy, is it not possible that we could impact our overall health based on how we interact with this energy? Close your eyes for a moment and imagine yourself pulling a very large magnet off your fridge door. Now imagine yourself as this magnet. The very thought you are having at this very moment is emitting energy in the form of a vibration. Anger or happiness, you are the master of your own feelings based on the dominating thoughts you have at this very moment. Every second of every day you have the choice of what vibration you want to send out, knowing you will only receive in return a similar vibration. Think of yourself as that giant fridge magnet sending out a very large magnetic field. Your thoughts are sending out a frequency into this magnetic field that is either negative or positive. This means you will attract back the same exact frequency you send out. If you think negative, you will receive only negative results back. This reality has either very positive or very damaging consequences on every result in your life, be it friends, family, relationships, finances or health – and it all starts with your current thought you are having RIGHT NOW.

Most of my 60,000 thoughts a day were very negative back when I was sick and unhealthy at the age of 26. My dominant thoughts would play over and over again in my mind. A few examples of my then-typical thoughts sounded something like this:

Why can't I be healthy?

I don't know what to do?

I'm no good at doing this!

Why does this always happen to me?

It is negative thoughts like the ones above that led me to experiencing constant feelings of anger, guilt, shame, frustration and sadness. My results were a direct link to my inability to feel happy, joy and excitement. I am not saying that I never felt happy. What I am saying is that my *dominant* thoughts were negative and as long as your dominant thoughts are negative, your results will be negative as well.

Think for a moment how your life would be different if your 60,000 thoughts a day were comprised of positive, uplifting and healthy intentions. It is your choice. You have the ability to shift your vibrations to attract positive results all by becoming more aware of how powerful your thoughts are to your results. When you combine positive thinking with healthier eating, your results magnify and become even easier to attain. Believe me, I did it for myself many years ago and now thousand of others are experiencing it as well.

YOUR VIBRATIONAL BUBBLE

Author Michael Losier in his book *Law of Attraction* explains it very well when he mentions that we all have a vibrational bubble. Michael says that it is our vibrational bubble that sends out signals to the Universe which automatically looks to match that signal. From experience, I could not agree more. What is your vibrational bubble made up of – mostly negative or mostly positive vibrations? The key is to set your vibrational bubble to 51% or higher with positive thoughts in order to manage the negatives. Just like with the *80/20 Rule* I introduced to you for eating more whole foods, the same works for your thoughts.

Unfortunately in modern North American society we are dominated with negative thoughts and therefore sending out negative vibrations. All you need to do is watch your local news report on TV or read a newspaper and you will discover what I am talking about.

Have you ever noticed that the dominating headline stories on TV and in your newspapers are about death and pain and people's unkind actions?

Being exposed to this daily doom and gloom used to leave me paralyzed in negativity before I even walked out the door. Today, I make a conscious effort to avoid reading the paper and watching the news as I am aware how it shifts my energy to the negative.

It's hard to notice the amazing flight of a bird or the delicate swaying of wild flowers in the wind when negatives dominate your mind.

My morning ritual of negatives would continue once I left home. I would walk out my front door carrying my negative vibes like baggage into the car and proceed to spend a good hour in traffic going to work. Morning traffic did nothing to help my negative thoughts, which would turn my feelings into anger and frustration the minute I hit a red light. The radio in my car ensured I wouldn't have a break from hearing more bad news. Followed my wake up blues, bad news and snail traffic, piles of papers always waited for me at work. All combined, it made sense why I was drenched in negative thoughts by 10 am. And I was eating foods that only left me low in energy and grumpy. As you can imagine, by this point my vibrational bubble was so negative that I was entangled in unhappy and unhealthy thoughts for the rest of the day. Most of my day's results where doomed the minute I opened my eyes in the morning.

Does any of this sound familiar? It might not be the exact same routine, but the main triggers for negative thoughts are common for many of us. What are your triggers? What sends you into feelings of anger, guilt and frustration?

We are all made up of energy and our thoughts emit a vibration. You know that now. It is in this scientifically-proven reality that your ability to gain abundant health lies. The impact your thoughts have on your health is far more significant than you can imagine.

If this is the case, what can you do to make sure you wake up each morning and set your vibration to a positive frequency and therefore attract positive results? The answer lies in your ability to disrupt your negative thought patterns. Your actions have been ingrained in you through years of habitual patterns. It is time to throw a curve ball into the mix and begin experiencing what it is like to bring positive vibrations into your life.

The key is to begin the shift the minute you open your eyes each and every morning. This is where I created what I call *My First Ten*, my system for producing spectacular results in everything you set your mind to – and **this only takes the first ten minutes of every day**.

I credit *My First Ten* to enhancing my ability to attracting a life of purpose and joy. Having lost over 40 pounds and reversing my pre-diabetic state, I no longer suffer through one-dimensional solutions and live each day with abundant happiness. This is a far cry from my bouts of depression I lived through many years ago. *My First Ten* is my system for attracting positive thoughts and is your starting point (along with following the *80/20 Rule* introduced to you during the first element, FOOD) where you will begin to experience unbelievable, life-long, healthy results the minute you put it into action.

So what do you need to know to get started? If you are ready for abundant happiness, keep reading....

SUCCESS SYSTEM #2 - MY FIRST TEN

How you begin the first ten minutes of each day is your entrance point to creating a healthier, stronger, happier you. From this day forward you will have no more excuses. It is your turn to shine and practicing *My First Ten* daily will help make it happen. *My First Ten* is designed to ease you into resetting your vibrational bubble from negative to positive each morning. Your success lies in getting out of bed each morning and spending the first ten minutes of your day engaging any one or a combination of *My First Ten* exercises, which I share with you below. Each exercise is designed to produce positive thoughts, which will create healthy feelings, resulting in uplifting actions, ending in your amazing results. This may sound a bit out of the ordinary to you, but I promise, if you practice *My First Ten* on a daily basis, you will be witness to your own evolution and it all starts with your first thought of each day.

The key here is to realize that you only need to spend ten minutes in order to shift your vibration for the entire day. There is no pressure to do any more unless you choose to.

During your ten minutes be aware of your surroundings and be as present as possible. At first it might be challenging, but it will get easier. At the conclusion of your *My First Ten* practice I want you to be aware of your thoughts as you continue on with your daily routine. Any time you are met with a challenge and your thoughts turn negative, take three deep breaths and place yourself back into your morning practice and connect to the positive feelings you were experiencing then. This will reset your vibration back to positive and help you move through your day with ease. Sounds too easy to be true? Well, it is true. No pill to pop, no special diet to follow, just you and your thoughts, that's the key to true happiness and abundant health. Give it a try and see for yourself.

Below is a list of your *My First Ten* exercises. These are the same exercises I practiced to gain back control over my own health and continue to practice daily to prevent disease and maintain my life of living from joy and happiness.

Some of these exercises will resonate strongly with you and others will not. That is okay. Please feel free to add on any number of your own exercises that help you to enter into a state of positive energy. I would also welcome you sharing any exercises you feel may benefit others to achieve abundant health. Please email me your experience with *My First Ten* as well as any exercises you would like to share and I will spread the word.

YOUR 3 STEPS TO SUCCESS

There are 3 key steps to ensuring you maximize your potential while practicing *My First Ten*.

1. PERSONAL SPACE

Ideally, you will create a safe space that is quiet and comfortable where you will not be disturbed during your practice. Find your personal space where you can begin to build your daily *My First Ten* practice. Your ideal space is somewhere where you can post materials on the walls and be free of distractions.

2. BE PREPARED

Although each morning you may choose different exercises, having all the tools, materials and equipment on hand will ensure you continue on with your practice each morning. Be sure to gather all your materials needed to engage in your practice. Once you have all your materials on hand, you will be prepared to practice *My First Ten* every day without anything holding you back.

3. TAKE CARE OF BUSINESS

If there are a few things you *need* to do in order to be fully present during your *My First Ten* practice, it is best to take care of it before your practice. Take a shower, wash your face or brush your teeth – these are acceptable. Getting a cup of coffee is not. It is important that you begin your daily practice as soon as possible each morning. Being aware of this, you be the judge of your starting point.

IT'S TIME TO BEGIN

The top 6 exercises are the most important ones to include in your *My First Ten* practice and have been a part of my practice from many years. These first 6 exercises have allowed me to manifest amazing results with my health, relationships and business. Many of my results I experienced within days of starting to practice *My First Ten* while others took just weeks or only a few months. I promise you that you too can experience amazing results as long as you really want it and are ready to make it a reality.

EXERCISES FOR *MY FIRST TEN*

BREATHE

Breathing is vital to life and is at the top of the list of things most of us take for granted. Are you a shallow breather? Do you often find yourself holding your breath without even knowing it? Breathing is essential to longevity and the deeper you

breathe the longer you will live. It truly is that simple.

So how do you go about shifting the way you breathe? It's all about awareness. Ideally you will be utilizing your breath during every practice of *My First Ten*, but it is essential to take the breath with you throughout your entire day. Your breath is the number one point of entrance into shifting your vibrational bubble. Whenever you begin to feel tense in any way, it's time to connect to your breath and relieve the tension before it brings about negative vibrations.

Here is a simple 3-step breathing exercise you can utilize to bring calmness into your daily *My First Ten* practice as well as throughout your day.

1. Begin by taking a long, slow, deep breath in and feel the air filling your entire lungs.
2. Once your lungs are full, hold your breath for 1 second and feel the tension release.
3. Finish off by slowly exhaling all the air in your lungs and repeat two more times.

Taking 3 deep breaths will allow you to quickly feel calmness and help you reset your energy to a more positive vibration. Your breath is a great way to start and finish each and every *My First Ten* daily practice.

MEDITATION

Historically meditation has shown to provide numerous health benefits such as reduced stress, improve mental clarity, increase oxygen flow and pain reduction, to name just a few. Meditation has increased in popularity in North America over the past decade as more and more people search for a way to decrease life's hectic pace.

I will admit that at first meditation was very difficult for me, but I have since discovered the true benefits of practicing daily. There is a reason it is part of the top 6 exercises I recommend for including in your *My First Ten* practice. Along with breathing, meditation is the number one point of entrance for shifting your energy.

HELPFUL STEPS FOR MEDITATION

1. **Find a comfortable spot to sit.** You may choose to use a cushion or block to sit up on. You can even use a chair if you wish.

2. **Sit quietly and begin to observe your breathing**. Most likely your thoughts will begin to race. This is normal. Allow your thoughts to flow gently. Don't pay too close attention to them and they will pass. It is the mind's nature to think, so do not try and turn the mind off. In time you will be able to slow it down and eventually control the flow of thoughts, enhancing your meditation experience.

3. **Focus on your breath**. Become aware of your breathing. It is in your breathing that you reach the point of entrance to shifting your vibration. Focus on the movement of air flowing in and out of your body.

4. **Simply be present** with what is taking place within you. If you become distracted by outer sounds or inner thoughts, just refocus on your breath.

5. **When closing your meditation practice** slowly open your eyes. Take a moment to ground yourself to the experience. When ready, gently lift yourself to a standing position and carry on

with another *My First Ten* exercise or carry on with your day.

There are many books, classes or free online guided meditations you can explore to enhance your experience or help get you started. The key to meditation is understanding that there is no right or wrong. There is only do and you will succeed.

VISUALIZATION

The mind is the most powerful part of you. It is not what your eyes see, but what your mind creates for your eyes to see that is true brilliance manifested. Many years ago I would have thought this was a ridiculous concept, but today, I know it is the truth. The sooner you believe, the sooner you will experience lasting healthy results.

In order to experience the true power of visualizing, you need to use your imagination. Your imagination is more powerful then many of us realize. Each of us creates our own reality, consciously or unconsciously. Either you choose to imagine and thereby move in the direction of your dreams or you accept life as it comes, seemingly unaware of your endless ability to control and shape your life.

When you visualize it is important that you see it, imagine it, feel it as if you are truly experiencing it at that moment. If you practice visualization with full complete awareness and belief, I promise, you will being to manifest in your life all you desire.

One of the greatest benefits to visualizing is its ability to put you into a state of relaxation, where you replenish and re-energize, while keeping your vision alive and thriving.

Visualizing does not require a lot of time. Even a one minute visualization session will produce amazing results. The more you practice visualizing, the easier it gets to enter into a state of deep relaxation where you then create your vision with the help of your imagination, exactly as you desire.

As you practice, be aware of the energy pouring over and through you. This is your connection to the Universe and sharing in this energy will manifest your vision at a higher level. Sometimes I can't believe I am talking this way, coming from a place of being overweight, pre-diabetic and depressed for many years – yet this is why

I can honestly share this information with you, I know it works.

You can use the power of visualization to imagine your way to whatever you want. Nothing within the realm of human accomplishment is impossible to you. The one important addition to your ability to manifest your vision is to believe. The more you believe without a doubt and act as though whatever you want is on its way, the sooner you will experience your every desire.

VISION BOARD

Seeing it before your eyes can be very powerful. Visualization has the mind creating your desires for your eyes to see. With a vision board you are taking your desires and bringing them into the material world.

Ever wonder what it would look, feel, taste, touch, smell like, your dreams in reality, your life goals accomplished, your ideal life manifested all around you? Why not create this through pictures, words, images that represent who you want to become and how you want to live. Creating a vision board helps put attention, energy and focus on your goals and serves as a powerful reminder of what lies just around the corner if you want it. Clarity is important in order to achieve your life goals. A vision board helps to uncover many hidden gems that will create clarity in your desired goals and allow for a deeper connection during your visualization practice.

Here's how to create your very own vision board:

1. **Get Organized**. Find a box and place all your supplies into it. Markers, tape, glue stick, scissors, stickers and any other items you would like to use to be creative.

2. **Choose a Canvas**. Go to your local dollar store and purchase a poster board or canvas. Think of your personal *My First Ten* practice space. What size would fit your space to ensure there is still room for other *My First Ten* exercises, but not so small that your vision board is not visible to do its job.

3. **Find What You Desire**. Look through old magazines, newspapers, catalogs, photos and inspiring words from articles and begin cutting them out and preparing them for your vision board. The internet is also a wealth of possibilities for your vision board as well as

friends and family who might have old magazines to rummage through.

Cut out pictures, words and images that represent your dreams and desires. When choosing items, think about where you would like to see your life in 5 years, 2 years, six months from now or what your mind created for your eyes to see during your visualization. Most of my vision boards are based on what I imagined during my visualization sessions.

4. **Create Your Vision Board**. Feel free to create different vision boards based on certain themes in your life. I have one for my business and one for my family/friends/play life. You can even create vision boards based on times. One for six months from now and another for how your life will look in 10 years. You have complete freedom to create as you wish. Be proud of your choices and don't hold back from creating as grand as you possibly can. It is all possible if you believe.

Don't worry if your vision board does not look *exactly* as you desire. I have created several vision boards and

they always change as I achieve my goals and set new ones.

5. **Special Location**. You already have your space set for your *My First Ten* daily practice. This is the ideal location for you to hang your vision board. You may also wish to hang your vision board in another location. You may even choose to create multiple vision boards and place them in multiple locations. It is up to you where you hang your vision boards, but it is important that you make them a part of your daily practice.

6. **Reward your Eyes**. When you have hung your vision board it is now a part of you. Take as little as 30 seconds during you're *My First Ten* practice and dive into your creation. What do you see in front of you? What have you put attention, energy and focus towards? If it is on your vision board, you can experience it. The more time you spend with your board the stronger you will omit an energy frequency out to the Universe that will attract your desires back to you. IT WORKS, I've done it many times. Just you reading this book proves it works. *e3 for LIFE* is one of

my main vision boards that I have used for the past two years during my *My First Ten* practice. It is still hanging there because I have not been on Oprah with my book yet, but it is coming even if she is retiring soon.

GRATITUDE

I define gratitude as a feeling of thankfulness or appreciation for something or someone in your life that in turn creates a positive emotion.

What are you most grateful for in your life at this moment?

Part of *My First Ten* daily practice is spending 2 minutes listing the 5 things I am most grateful for in my life right now. I call this *My Grateful Daily 5*. When I first began practicing *My Grateful Daily 5,* I was coming up with the same things every day.

I am grateful for my wife Suzie
I am grateful for my Family
I am grateful for my Health
I am grateful for my Friends
I am grateful for my Business

It is OK to have the same 5 everyday if it still creates the feeling of gratitude. Over my practice I have learnt to break down *My Grateful Daily 5* to heighten the emotion created and enhance the energy frequency I omit. The more detail you can create within each of your *My Grateful Daily 5*, the stronger your results will be. For example, one of my recent sessions looked like this:

- I am grateful for Suzie's beautiful smile, her amazing ability to make me happy and her ability to share her love without compromise.

- I am grateful for my niece Geri's super fun giggle, her small gentle hands wrapping around my shoulders as she jumps on my back and her energetic, care free spirit that brings a smile to my face with ease.

- I am grateful for feeling energized and for taking the time to consciously breathe throughout my day.

- I am grateful for being able to provide my friends with a passionate ear to listen and a willingness to be a source of support if needed.

- I am so grateful for my newest client who I have helped to experience more energy and increased happiness to ease him towards a healthier life.

It is all about the emotion you create during *My Grateful Daily 5*. I have learned to be grateful for just about anything in my life, because I now know that being grateful is the fastest way to create a positive feeling. As you already know, your feelings create your actions and your actions lead to every result you have. Being grateful means healthier, happier results.

ENGAGING *MY GRATEFUL DAILY 5*

Create a gratitude journal that you can keep in your private *My First Ten* practice space. Each morning during your *My First Ten* practice, spend 2 minutes and write down your *My Grateful Daily 5*. Writing them down will strengthen the emotion created and allow you to look back on past lists to reenergize as needed. Next time you are feeling a little depressed or stressed, just go into your *My First Ten* space and read a past *My Grateful Daily 5* list. This will reset your energy and allow you to eliminate any unwanted negative vibrations.

Your ability to be grateful begins with a thought and ends with an emotion. No matter how you engage your *My Grateful Daily 5,* whether written down in your gratitude journal or explored with your eyes closed, as long as you create the emotion, you will be releasing any negative vibrations and filling your energy bank where only positive results can manifest.

There are only two ways to live your life. One is as though nothing is a miracle. The other is as though everything is a miracle.
~ Albert Einstein

Throughout your day try to bring *My Grateful Daily 5* into play. I carry around a little strawberry shortcake doll (2 inches tall) in my pocket. It reminds me of my niece Geri. Any time I feel it in my pocket it automatically brings a smile to my face and resets my energy to positive. The more you can remove the negative and bring in the positive energy throughout your day, the easier your results come.

CELEBRATION

Celebration is another amazing way to increase your ability to manifest all your life's dreams. Your ability to bring celebration into your daily life begins during your *My First Ten* practice. The minute you finish visualizing – celebrate; when you have completed each of your *My Gratitude Daily 5* – celebrate; when you take a look at your vision board and see all that is coming – celebrate. No matter how small the accomplishment, celebrate it as if it was the greatest thing that has every happened.

Why celebrate? Celebration is another way to create a feeling of being grateful and as you now know, being grateful removes the negative and brings the positive.

There are many ways to celebrate. I have utilized many celebration techniques over the years, but none have worked better than a good old fashion fist pump in the air with a big yahoo! Give it a try right now. It's amazing how quickly a fist pump and yahoo will bring a smile to your face and reset your energy to positive. Did you try it? Try it now with me...... YAHOOO! Doesn't that feel awesome?

Get creative in your celebrations. Don't be shy. Even if someone sees you, pay no attention, it's worth the rewards. One of my favorite celebration techniques is carrying around a party horn in my jacket pocket. Whenever I feel the need to celebrate, I pull it out and create a mini celebration party. Yes, I get some stares at restaurants or passing vehicles, but the smile on my face is contagious and soon others are joining in. It's amazing how many people want to celebrate, but are too embarrassed to show their true feelings of joy.

I promise that if you release your joy through celebration, you will experience a level of happiness that will manifest all your desires. Take a look around you right now. What do you see or have in your life worth celebrating? Even the smallest things are worth a fist pump in the air and a big yahoo. As odd as this may sound, celebration sets your vibration to positive and only brings you more positive results in return, while allowing you to feel fantastic.

To celebrate is to tell the Universe you are ready for more, so celebrate, celebrate, celebrate.

The following exercises below are all part of *My First Ten* and should be included, as you feel fit. Although they are not as crucial as the first 6, they play an equal role in removing your negative energy and resetting your vibration to positive. Feel free to include any number of these exercises into your *My First Ten* daily practice as well as to come up with your own that help shift your energy frequency.

POST POSITIVE SAYINGS

Post positive, uplifting sayings or re-minders around your *My First Ten* practice space. Some of the sayings I have posted include the following:

I Love You

Breathe

Lots can happen in one day,
in one week, in one month

Our only limitations are those we set up
in our own minds

Nothing has meaning
except the meaning I give it

Today I will become
a better version of myself

Celebrate all wins

How I do anything
is how I do everything

It only takes a matter of seconds to read one of your sayings and every time you read one it will create a stronger positive vibration.

EXERCISE

I can't say enough about regular fitness and is worthy of an entire book on its own, but for the intentions of *My First Ten*, spending 2 minutes on an optimal fitness routine such as doing a series of jumping jacks, push-ups and sit-ups, will get your blood moving and your oxygen flowing. Search the internet and come up with the ideal short program that suits your ability and setting, and just do it. You will find the more you include even the smallest amount of fitness into your *My First Ten* practice, the more you will want to seek out other times in your day to experience the rewards that come from regular exercise.

STRETCH/YOGA

Same as with fitness, stretching/yoga is crucial for injury prevention as well as maintaining a limber and fit body and mind. Come up with your own 2-minute stretch/yoga routine. It's not about the length of time you spend doing it, it's about doing it. The more you stretch, the more you will crave finding more time to continue stretching. At first just make stretching a part of your *My First Ten* practice and then find other times in your day to increase your time spent stretching or practicing yoga.

PREPARE TO EAT

On of my personal favorite exercises to do during *My First Ten* is to get into my kitchen and prepare a healthy breakfast, lunch or dinner. It is amazing what happens when you consciously take an active role in preparing your food. When I say active, I mean being present as you pick out each ingredient and take care and give thanks as you use each ingredient. Giving thanks has nothing to do with being religious, it is the idea that you are filling your food with positive energy so that it may provide you with the essentials needed for optimal health. So much of my past life was spent just eating. Now I give thanks to my food for what it provides and in return I feel powerful, energized and fulfilled while eating.

When it comes time to eat, you will appreciate your food so much more and put yourself in a state of gratitude during every bite. It is extremely important that during this time you are as present as possible with everything you see, smell, taste, touch and hear to be sure to enjoy and savor the eating process.

Here is a little exercise to try that you can bring into your *My First Ten* practice with any food ingredient. You can even use this with a group of friends to share the experience of being present with food. Try it next time you are out for dinner with the family. It is called "I Love Spinach" but can be used with any ingredient.

I LOVE SPINACH EXERCISE

This exercise is based on engaging spinach with your 5 senses: see, touch, smell, taste and hear. I want you to go into your *My First Ten* practice space and take 15 seconds on each sense. Some with eyes open, most with eyes closed. That is a total of 75 second, not very long at all for what is to come for you. Once you begin, don't stop until all your 5 senses are engaged. Here is how to do this exercise.

FOLLOW THESE STEPS

1. **See**. With your eyes open, spend 15

seconds and just look at your piece of spinach and notice everything you see. What do you notice? What color is it? What is its shape? How about size?

2. **Touch.** With your eyes closed, spend the next 15 seconds to become familiar with how your piece of spinach feels. Pay special attention to the texture of the spinach, the shape, edges. What do you notice about it?

3. **Smell**. With your eyes closed, spend the next 15 seconds and smell your piece of spinach. I want you to really breathe it in. Place it right up to your nose and take in the aroma. What do you notice, is it sweet, does it have an earthy tone?

4. **Taste.** With your eyes closed, spend the next 15 seconds with the piece of spinach in your mouth and really taste it. I want you to take this part very slow. Really acknowledge each time you chew. What do you notice? Does it have more flavor than you expected? Is it a bit chewier than you thought it would be? Really be present as you take it in.

5. **Hear**. With your eyes closed, spend the last 15 seconds just being present to what you hear. What sounds do you hear around you? How about your own internal sounds of chewing or swallowing? Just recognize all the sounds around and inside of you.

Now open your eyes slowly and take 3 deep breaths.

This exercise will not only bring you amazing satisfaction as you learn to become more present with your food, but it will reconnect you to your relationship with food. I use this exercise during many of my corporate wellness events and it's amazing what participants experience. Try adding a new ingredient every few days during your *My First Ten* practice and become amazed at what you experience.

ART

If you like to paint, draw, color, sculpt, paper-mâché, stencil, or any other creative activity, this is an amazing opportunity to bring your attention, energy and focus into your creation. What a peaceful way to start your day. Spend just a few minutes during your *My First Ten* practice adding on to a piece of art you have begun or start a new one from scratch. The health benefits of being creative are endless and will set your vibration to positive with ease.

No more excuses – pick up that paint brush or pencil and begin. You only need to spend a few minutes each morning and the feeling of accomplishment will be with you the rest of your day.

This works the same for music. If you are a musician or just starting out learning a new instrument, this is your time to spend a few minutes exploring the amazing sounds you can create through music. Don't hesitate, pick up that banjo (that's me talking to myself to finally include my banjo into my practice) and begin experiencing the pleasure of making music.

ATTITUDES OF HEALTH

I created a list that I call my *Attitudes of Health*. I recite this list every morning during my practice of *My First Ten*. Here it is for you to see.

ATTITUDES OF HEALTH
- I create my life. I create a level of health that keeps me energetic and stress free.

- I am an excellent controller of my own health.
- I believe health is important, health is freedom and health makes life more enjoyable.
- I always put my health first.
- My part-time business is managing my health and investing my time creating a strong and vibrant body.
- I get healthy doing what I love.
- I deserve to be healthy because I add value to other people's lives.
- My capacity to strengthen and grow my health expands day by day.

Feel free to use the same *Attitudes of Health* or come up with your own list that gets your energy flowing with positive vibrations. It can even be a list based on your business or relationships.

I posted my *Attitudes of Health* beside my vision board on my wall where I practice *My First Ten*. When I recite my *Attitudes of Health* I place my hand over my heart and say each one out loud with meaning so that I feel the vibration rushing though my heart. It is an amazing exercise and takes less then 30 seconds to do.

You can visit www.PowerofFood.com

to download a free copy of my *Attitudes of Health*.

DANCE

Yes, I love to dance to some of my favorite music while practicing *My First Ten*. There is no way I would have felt comfortable admitting that a few years ago, but now I know the benefits of letting loose and dancing free.

During my last dance session I jumped around my practice space smiling and singing to *Here Comes the Sun* by the Beatles.

It only takes a few seconds of dancing to bring a smile to your face and a open heart for receiving healthy, positive vibrations. At first it might feel a bit strange – trust me, I know. Keep on dancing during your *My First Ten* practice and you will feel lighter and more youthful when you walk out to start your day.

YOUR DAILY AFFIRMATION

Right beside my *Attitudes of Health* and above my vision board lays my daily affirmation. An affirmation is a statement asserting the existence or the truth of something. I only have one affirmation and I recite it three times at the conclusion of my daily practice of *My First Ten*. Do you want to know what it is?

Everything is in place.
The Universe is here to serve me.
I am free to run.

I believe without a doubt that the Universe is here to serve me and that everything is in place for me to experience the life of my dreams. It is in my ability to take action and face my fears to ensure I manifest everything I desire. I would not have thought this way back when I was sick and unhealthy, but having seen results first hand, I will never doubt the power of my mind.

What do you believe in without a doubt? Is there something you know to be true and want to strengthen within your life? It is the creation of your affirmation that will empower you to bring it to your consciousness and allow it to become reality.

JOURNALING

Are you a writer? Have you always wanted to put words to paper? Even if you have never tried it before, journaling can be an amazing exercise worthy of spending a few minutes during your *My First Ten* practice. Write a poem; share your story of who you will be today; how about starting an article for a local paper or magazine? You are in complete control and have the freedom to explore in any way you wish.

I have a specific journal in my practice space that I keep available for moments when I feel inspired to write. Although it is not a regular exercise for me during my practice, I find it very satisfying when I do explore journaling.

picture to the possibilities that lie ahead for you? You have now been introduced to two of the three elements for attaining optimal health. Within the chapter on FOOD, I shared with you the *80/20 Rule* and over 60 recipes to make it easy for you to reach the *Magic Number* of 51%. It was during the last chapter on THOUGHTS where you discovered *My First Ten* and how easy it can be to set your energy to positive. Now it is time to introduce you to the final element for attaining abundant health and happiness with ease. That element is HABITS.

YOU NOW HAVE THE POWER

Now you have the power to start each day emitting a positive vibration. Your daily *My First Ten* practice will set your energy frequency in the right direction to ensure you live your life on your terms, with the health you want and the vitality you deserve.

How are you doing? Are you tuning into what I have shared with you so far? Does it resonate with you? Is it painting a clear

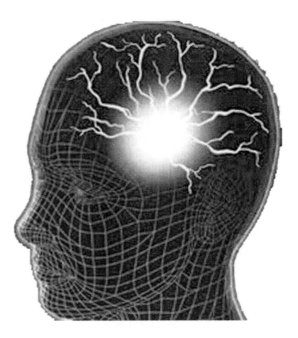

PART 4

HABITS

YOUR HABITS HAVE POWER

You are here, reading this, for a reason. There is something you want. Something you would like to have different with your health. Something in your life is holding you back from experiencing abundant health and happiness everyday.

Our junk habits such as eating late at night, overeating, eating too quickly and eating all the wrong foods are all caused by a rooted pattern in our daily actions that have led to the formation of our limiting habits. In the case of one-dimensional solutions, we don't experience a shift in the root cause of our junk habits. Dieting is a perfect example of this. Many diets do not create the necessary shift at the root level of your daily actions and eventually many of us fail. Not addressing the underlying problem leads to a large percentage of dieters gaining the weight back when finished as well as a large percentage gaining *more* weight than before the diet started. In this section of *e3 for LIFE*, I will reveal to you my system for getting to the roots of your unhealthy, junk habits – it is a system that

will easily allow you to bring in healthier habits without restrictions to your diet or lifestyle while you simultaneously engage the *80/20 Rule* for FOOD and *My First Ten* with your THOUGHTS. This system is called *Break That Habit.*

YOUR JUNK HABITS

Engaging your junk habits in a new way through utilizing the *Break That Habit* system will complement what you have already discovered through the first two e3

elements to attaining abundant health and happiness, **FOOD** and **THOUGHTS**.

As discussed earlier, we have on average 60,000 thoughts per day. Each of these 60,000 *thoughts* leads to a *feeling* you have. This *feeling* creates an *action* you take. It is in these *actions* that your *habits* are formed. The *habits* you have, have created every *result* you now experience in your life, whether it is friends, family, business or health – and it all started with a single thought.

The missing link in your ability to achieve amazing results with your health is in your *awareness* between your daily actions and how your mind response to your actions.

For example, imagine putting a piece of chocolate into your mouth. What is your usual response?

What about going to the gym, what thoughts and feelings does that bring up for you?

Every result you have is directly related to how it makes you feel. If you experience pain, most of us will do anything we can to avoid it. We want to experience pleasure, not pain, and food is our number one pleasure source in our society.

Many of you spend hundreds or even thousands of dollars each year on diets, being on cleanses, buying gym memberships, taking supplements or prescription drugs all to try and attain better health.

Most of the time these solutions only bring us right back to the same health state where we started. This is because many of our solutions do not get to the roots of why we do what we do, why we take the actions we take each and every day. Every day you take hundreds and hundreds of actions. These actions are what get you through your days.

As I have mentioned before, but want to stress once again, it is your daily actions that you take over and over again that create the habits you currently have.

Do you see what I am getting at? Is this resonating with you? Am I painting a clear picture?

Most of our solutions we chose when trying to feel and look better, provide unsustainable results. Even if we do experience a positive result, they are quite often short-lived and we are right back to the same old experience.

I know this first hand. I have been on several diets in the past and they only led me to feeling angry, frustrated or guilty be-cause I went back to the same old results soon after I finished each diet. When we feel angry, sad, frustrated or guilty, what kind of results do you get? You know what these results look like. Most dieting only brings about experiencing the same results over and over again.

What happens if you restrict yourself from something?

I would like you to close your eyes for a moment. Now with your eyes closed I want you to take five seconds and imagine you are going into your fridge or cupboard and reaching for your one favorite comfort food. Now you have it in your hand and you slowly put it into your mouth and take a bite.

How does this feel for you? Are you ex-periencing the pleasure right now? What is your favorite comfort food?

Mine happens to be shortbread cookies – the salt, sugar and fat are hard to let go.

We all have our favorite comfort foods. How would you feel if you could never eat that food again? I know for me that is out of the question. Every time I wanted to get healthier in the past I relied on solutions that restricted me in one way or another. I am happy to tell you that you do not have to restrict yourself in any way to get healthier. In fact, it is more important to your health that you don't restrict yourself if you are going to experience long term success with your health and happiness.

What happens if something you want to achieve is not easy?

PAIN VS. PLEASURE

Most North Americans want their results quick and simple and if it is not quick and simple, we tend to not do anything. Pain vs. pleasure. What makes me so successful as a coach is that *quick and simple, without restrictions* are the corner stones of everything I teach.

Do you want your results quick and simple? Of course, we all do.

Each of you has that same power within you to get the results you desire. You just need to release it and I am going to reveal to you the system I used, which will make it easy for you to experience similar amaz-ing results as what I achieved over the past 10 years. In fact what you have discovered in the pages of *e3 for LIFE* took me over

10 years to discover. I am very happy to be sharing this with you and eliminating your need for spending countless hours, energy and money to figure it all out.

After your learn the *Break That Habit* system, and use it in conjunction with the *80/20 Rule* and *My First Ten*, you will have no more excuses, no more self-sabotaging. You will be in complete control of your own health and happiness.

I am now going to introduce you to *Break That Habit*. In combination with the *80/20 Rule* and *My First Ten*, *Break That Habit* will transform your junk habits from negative anchors holding you down to uplifting daily achievements you will thrive on.

Once your habit forms it is either positive or negative. Strengthen the ones that support, and take action on the ones that hold you back. That is what I wish to help you with.

Break That Habit is a simple-to-follow, easy-to-implement, self-guided program that, if followed daily, will propel you to long term success while inviting new, fresh, healthy habits to form. Combined with your new awareness of the first two e3 elements for abundant health and happiness, FOOD and THOUGHTS, engaging your HABITS with ease, will allow you to experience all you desire.

SO WHAT YOUR SAYING IS IF I EAT BETTER FOOD, CHANGE MY BAD HABITS, AND THINK MORE POSITIVE THOUGHTS, I WILL BE HEALTHIER?

SUCCESS SYSTEM #3 - BREAK THAT HABIT

The *Break That Habit* system is designed to make it easy for you to reduce the impact your limiting junk habits are having on your overall health. The system is based on the idea that once you start becoming aware of the impact of your daily actions on your overall health, you can begin to shift the impact these actions have to a more positive outcome.

Several years ago I realized that I had a number of limiting, junk habits that were contributing to my already declining health. Being 40 pounds overweight, suffering from high cholesterol, anxiety attaches, ADHD, stress, food allergies, asthma and pre-diabetic, I began to realize that my multiple junk habits were a major factor in my declining health. I did not want to live an unhealthy life any longer and after years of diets, supplements, cleanses and prescription drugs, I decided to start taking action towards regaining control over my own health. While researching all about the healing power of food I began looking into effective ways to overcome obstacles.

My research led me to creating a habit-busting system for myself called *Break That Habit*.

It was this system in combination with reconnecting to my relationship with the food I ate as well as engaging my energy through my thoughts, that allowed me to lose over 40 pounds, reverse my pre-diabetic state, lower my cholesterol and live each day with abundant health and happiness. I know you can experience the same results.

You can begin the *Break That Habit* system through engaging your own *Personal Habit Effect*. Once you have done this initial step, you will be on your way.

YOUR PERSONAL HABIT EFFECT

We all struggle in similar ways with our health. You now know that many of us rely on solutions that don't get to the roots of why we do what we do. Why do you take actions you know are going to cause your health harm? You take them because they provide comfort. What a strange concept! We do things to ourselves that cause us harm and we do so because they provide comfort.

Let me give you an example of how we do things that cause harm, but give us pleasure at the same time. I have a friend Suzanne who is the sweetest person in the world. She would not hurt a fly. Suzanne loves to watch *American Idol* on television.

Suzanne has a ritual every week when *American Idol* comes on where she sets up a mini table beside her couch with her favorite comfort foods for the night. On the table she has salted crackers with a side of cream cheese, a bag of potato chips with salsa and a box of gummy bears. She usually drinks a diet coke.

On several occasions Suzanne has called me from work the next morning after watching *American Idol*, because she is feeling depressed. For the longest time she did not link how she felt to her *American Idol* ritual, but I began to notice her pattern and got her to create her own *Personal Habit Effect* list.

Upon completing her list, Suzanne dis-covered that many of her junk habits oc-curred while watching television and she realized that her depression was most se-vere the mornings after she ate all her com-fort food while watching TV.

Over the course of the next month Su-zanne struggled with changing her *American Idol* ritual. She had no idea how power-ful the comfort was in her habits. She tried to stop bringing food in front of the televi-sion, but she found this change very pain-ful. So she decided to just let it be and be-gan telling herself, **"Everything is Okay."**

Saying *"everything is okay"* has very dangerous implications to your health! Essentially when you say *"everything is okay,"* it means you are giving up and tak-ing the easy way out of having to do some-thing about the way you feel. There is only so long you can fool yourself by saying *"everything is okay"* before you end up sick – whether it's obesity, diabetes, can-cer or heart disease. I used to say it all the time and I am sure you know someone, if not yourself, who says it often. Most of the time we don't even know we say it. Say-ing *"everything is okay"* provides comfort. Doing something about your health causes pain, unless there is a simple way to do it.

That is what *e3 for LIFE* is all about, making it simple for you to stop saying *"everything is okay"* and begin thriving with ease.

The next time Suzanne called me I suggested having me be her coach for 30 days. Suzanne hadn't quite accepted the idea of coaching. I have told her how much success my clients have been having making healthy shifts with ease, but she still refused to give it a try. So as a friend I decided to provide her with some friendly advice. I told her that if she restricted herself in any way, there was no way she would find success in trying to reduce the impact of her unhealthy habits. I suggested to not eliminate anything from her nighttime ritual, but to instead decrease her portions while watching *American Idol* and include one healthy snack that offered some nutritional value to complement her comfort foods. No restrictions.

Suzanne took my advice and the next time she sat to watch *American Idol* she took only half the crackers, half the chips and half the gummy bears and included some chopped vegetables. Over the course of one month Suzanne implemented my friendly advice and slowly removed the junk food and continued to bring in healthier options. She would send me a morning email every few days to tell me how much happier she was feeling about herself and how much more energy she now had. I know this might sound too easy, but it works!

On our last conversation, Suzanne was overwhelmed with a feeling of gratitude. She was so surprised that her shift in energy and happiness was coming so quickly and easily. By not eliminating anything from her routine (what I call the darkness), Suzanne began to bring in healthier options (what I call sources of light). How does this feel for you? Are you getting the picture? Do you see what I am getting at?

What I told Suzanne, I am now sharing with you. When you start to look at your limiting junk habits you must begin by taking very small, daily action steps to improve the impact your limiting junk habits have on your overall health, without restrictions. It is important to keep each and every action steps as small as possible without reaching too high too fast. This will ensure you are able to succeed more often and enjoy celebrating your successes daily. That means not taking away all the cookies and chips, but cutting the portions down a little and adding a few whole foods into the mix.

There is a comfort in your habits, even the ones that cause damage to your health. By engaging your *Personal Habit Effect* you too can begin to experience a lighter more energized life without restrictions to your diet or lifestyle. Below I share with you the steps to follow once you have completed your *Personal Habit Effect* to ensure you quickly and easily begin to achieve the results you desire. But first I want to share with you my own *Personal Habit Effect* list from back when I was sick and unhealthy.

On the next page I provide you with my very own *Personal Habit Effect* list. Creating this list allowed me to begin to develop a strategy for reducing the impact these habits were having on my health. Very soon you will fill out your own *Personal Habit Effect* and begin to take action for a healthier you.

On page 173 is a list of my junk habits when I was pre-diabetic, overweight and very unhealthy.

STEP 1: YOUR PERSONAL HABIT EFFECT LIST

In a few moments you will list your *Personal Habit Effect*. Once you have completed this list you are ready to get started. This list is all your limiting junk habits that hold you back from abundant health and happiness. They are food related, but can also include any other junk habits you know are impacting your health. Now it is your turn. On the worksheet provided on page 174, write out your own *Personal Habit Effect* list.

If you do not want to write in your book, you can visit wwwPowerofFood.com and download your free *Personal Habit Effect Worksheet* to print off.

Now that you have finished your *Personal Habit Effect* list, you are ready to begin your *Break That Habit* program.

STEP 2: DAILY WORKSHEET

Now you need to begin engaging your junk habits daily. How you do this is by choosing two of your limiting junk habits from your *Personal Habit Effect* list and

PERSONAL HABIT EFFECT

Let's Get Started

The combination of our individual junk habits, also know as our *Person Habit Effect,* directly impacts our ability to be as healthy as possible. Once we begin to engage our junk habits, we can start to improve our overall wellbeing.

Below is a list of my junk habits when I was pre-diabetic, overweight and very unhealthy

MY PERSONAL HABITS • THE EXAMPLE SHOWN WAS MY PERSONAL HABIT EFFECT AT 26 YEARS OLD

 Example

1. I smoke

2. I rarely drink enough water

3. I don't get enough sleep

4. I watch too much TV

5. I eat too many chocolate bars and sweets

6. I hardly eat enough vegetables

7. I drink soda pop

8. I exercise very little

9. I am on too much medication

10. I drink a lot of beer

11. I drink coffee throughout the day

12. I overeat

13. I get very angry at co-workers

14. I am very stressed out all day

15. I never breath enough through my day

16. I eat too fast

17. I eat a lot of fast food

18.

19.

20.

⭐ Now it's your turn!
On the next page there is space provided for you to write down all your junk habits holding you back from better health

PERSONAL HABIT EFFECT

"EVERYDAY MAKE AN IMPROVEMENT"

Take the next 15 minutes and write out all your limiting junk habits.
Don't stop until you have at least 15 written down

1. _____
2. _____
3. _____
4. _____
5. _____
6. _____
7. _____
8. _____
9. _____
10. _____

11. _____
12. _____
13. _____
14. _____
15. _____
16. _____
17. _____
18. _____
19. _____
20. _____

When you start to look at your junk habits you can begin to take small, daily action steps to improve the impact they have on your overall health. It is important to keep each and every action steps as small as possible without reaching too high too fast. This will ensure you are able to succeed more often and enjoy celebrating your successes daily. That means no going out and jogging three miles when you haven't exercised for weeks. Start with a light walk around your block for 20 minutes and work up to the jog.

taking action to improve them everyday. I highly recommend engaging the *Break That Habit* system for as long as you have limiting junk habits, which is probably going to be a while. You will never eliminate all your limiting junk habits, but reducing the impact on your health is the goal. What you will notice as well is that as you begin to reduce the impact of your habits, new ones may emerge and as long as you are staying the course, practicing this system daily, they will not have nearly the same damaging impact they would otherwise. The habits you choose to work on are up to you. You can choose to spend an entire week focusing on your two most challenging habits or you can rotate between your entire *Personal Habit Effect* list of habits.

For example, on day one choose numbers 1 & 2 on your list, on day two choose numbers 3 & 4, on day three choose numbers 5 & 6 and so on. Once you have engaged each of your junk habits on your *Personal Habit Effect* list, start over again at 1 & 2. **No matter what you choose, stay the course by engaging at least two per day and see the results!**

Special feature: On the next page I have provided you with a look at the *Daily Success Steps Worksheet.* You are welcome to visit www.PowerofFood.com to download a free copy of the worksheet or you can order the entire *Break That Habit* 30-Day workbook to get started right away.

When you purchase your full *Break That Habit* program through www.PowerofFood.com, you will also receive the following additions to help track your progress and ensure you experience results within a matter of days:

1. 30 individual daily success worksheets.
2. Your weekly *Self-Guided Success Report Card* to track your results.
3. *Weekly Success Celebration Chart* – Here you will have an opportunity to list all your successes for the week, how taking your action steps made you feel, what is the next step for your continued success as well as a date tracker to plan your steps to success.
4. Weekly *PICK 2* – Your weekly *PICK 2* allows you to highlight your two standout successes of the week. By engaging your *PICK 2* you will further strengthen your resolve for continued success.
4. *Bringing in the Light* – This is your op-

DAILY SUCCESS STEPS
EXAMPLE

"TAKING ACTION IS THE KEY TO SUCCESS"

Begin each morning of the next 30 days by opening your workbook and filling in your name and date. Complete steps 1, 2 and 3 of your Daily Success Steps in the morning. Before going to bed each night complete steps 4 and 5. I have provided you with an example below.

DAY 1

___Adam Hart___
My Name

___January 1 2009___
Today's Date

Daily Success Steps

1. Declare Attitudes of Health

2. Choose 2 Habits to Conquer Today

3. Choose 1 Action Step per Habit

4. Acknowledge your Achievements

5. Daily Success Rating

DAILY ACTION STEP 1	*DAILY ACTION STEP 2*
Conquering Habit: Over eating	**Conquering Habit:** lack of exercise
Today's Action Step: today I will eat slower and only fill my plate with half of my normal potion size	**Today's Action Step:** today I will take a brisk walk around my block for at least 20 minutes
Once I accomplish this action step I will feel: less full all the time, in control over my eating habits, and not as tired after eating	**Once I accomplish this action step I will feel:** FANTASTIC, more energy, proud of myself, ready to do it again tomorrow

Acknowledge Your Daily Successes

Today I accomplished only eating half my normal portions for each meal and I took a 30 minute walk through my local park

Having achieved my daily action steps I feel very proud of myself, stronger and more in control over my bad habits. I FEEL HEALTHIER!

Daily Success Rating
For every action step you completed today shade in 1 star

⭐ ⭐

portunity to face your most challenging junk habits while building a foundation for quick and easy results with long term success.

Again, you can visit www.PowerofFood.com to download a free copy of your daily success worksheet or order the entire *Break That Habit* 30-Day program to get started right away. Whatever you choose to do, if you engage the *Break That Habit* system on a daily basis along with the *80/20 Rule* for FOOD and *My First Ten* for THOUGHTS, you are going to be unstoppable on your way to attaining abundant health and happiness.

BRINGING IT ALL TOGETHER

Now you know the *Break That Habit* system for beginning to engage your junk habits in a healthy way. I promise you that if you follow the system the way it is designed, it will provide you with a starting point for you to experience abundant health and happiness with ease. I know you can do it and I encourage you to visit www. PowerofFood.com if you need any support along the way.

So, now you have no more excuses, no more self sabotage is possible thanks to your new awareness of *e3 for LIFE*, the 3 elements for abundant health and happiness – FOOD, THOUGHTS & HABITS. What is your next move?

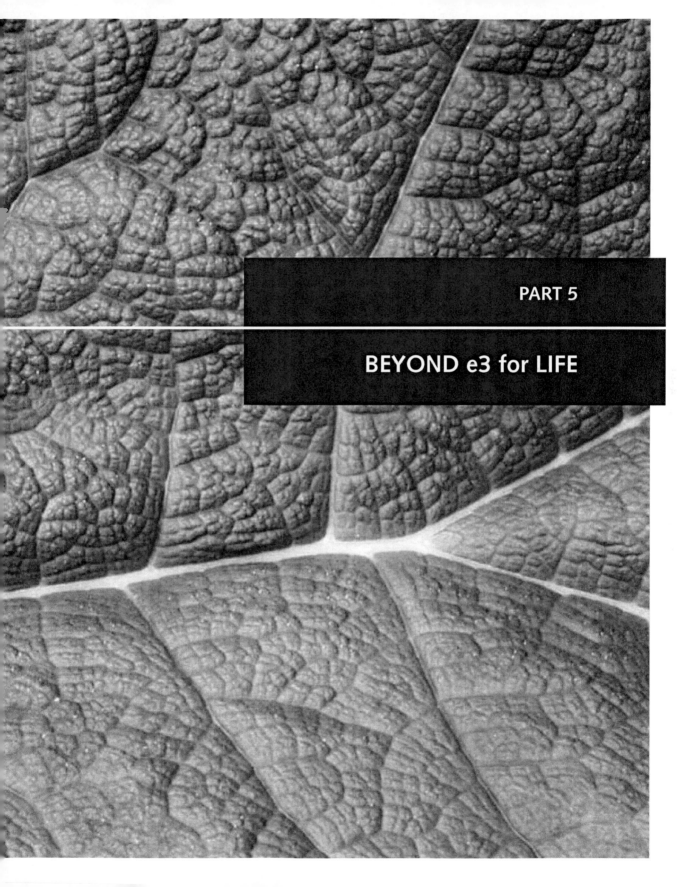

PART 5

BEYOND e3 for LIFE

5 STEPS TO MAKING YOUR RESULTS COUNT

Will this be another year where you wonder how it got to be the end of December and still you have not begun to take action towards losing those few pounds? How did it make you feel the last time you started a diet or exercise routine with great intentions, but only found yourself with the same results over and over again?

"I am going to lose 25 pounds in the next 6 months," or "I am going to start eating healthier food," and "I will begin an exercise routine that will boost my energy levels." Do any of these sound familiar? If so, it's time to make your results count!

I am one who knows from past experience it is not easy to achieve results unless you are willing to make an effort to ensure success. There is no quick fix and relying on one-dimensional solutions will only keep you locked in an unhealthy state. *e3 for LIFE* is your main resource for your continued drive towards better health.

Here are the 5 KEY STEPS to ensuring you stay the course and begin experiencing the results you desire within a matter of days.

Now that you have a clear understanding of *e3 for LIFE*, it is important to leave you with these 5 key steps that will help you to bring it all together.

1. SET YOUR INTENTION

First off you need to set your intentions. What is it you truly want? How would you like to feel everyday? Setting your intentions is the foundation to building a path for you experiencing abundant health and happiness. If I told you that doing this simple exercise is your key to unlocking everything you want in life, would you give it all your attention, energy and focus for the next few minutes? By setting your intentions, you will open up the floodgates for achieving amazing results.

Now it's up to you to detail on the next pages what it is you truly want in your life.

5 YEAR INTENTIONS

In as much detail as possible, what does your life look like 5 years from today?

1 YEAR INTENTIONS

In as much detail as possible, what does your life look like 1 year from today?

_____

_____

_____

_____

_____

_____

_____

_____

_____

_____

_____

_____

_____

_____

_____

_____

_____

_____

_____

_____

_____

_____

_____

30 DAY INTENTIONS

In as much detail as possible, what does your life look like 30 days from today?

_____

_____

_____

_____

_____

_____

_____

_____

_____

_____

_____

_____

_____

_____

_____

_____

_____

_____

_____

_____

_____

_____

_____

_____

2. MY FIRST TEN

Now that you have set your intentions, it is time to begin engaging your energy through practicing *My First Ten* which was introduced during the second of the e3 elements – THOUGHTS. Each of the *My First Ten* exercises will help to set your energy in a positive direction, ensuring your day is full of health and happiness.

3. TAKE ACTION

Now that you have set your intentions as well as begun practicing *My First Ten* daily, it is time to take action. It is in taking daily action that all your desired results become reality. The key to taking action is to make sure whatever you set out to achieve is possible. This means you must take very small daily action steps towards success. Following my *Break That Habit* system is your guide to easing you into achieving daily success through taking action. The more action steps you achieve, the more success you will experience; the more success you experience, the healthier and happier you will become – it is that simple.

4. CELEBRATE, CELEBRATE, CELEBRATE

Your intentions have been set, you are now practicing *My First Ten* daily and you are following the *Break That Habit* system for taking small daily action steps towards better health. Now it's time to celebrate, celebrate, celebrate!

Celebration is another key to manifesting all your life's goals. Every day you need to celebrate as much as possible. The minute you finish practicing *My First Ten* in the morning, celebrate. When you have completed each daily action step from your *Break That Habit* program, celebrate. When you see your kids playing outside, celebrate. Take a look around you right now and see all that you have in your life worth celebrating. Even the smallest things are worth a fist pump in the air and a big *yahoo!* As odd as this may sound, celebration is one of the quickest ways to reset your vibration to positive and bring you more positive results in return while making you feel amazing. I dare you to try it, RIGHT NOW!

5. GET SUPPORT

Overcoming your health challenges or life struggles can be very tough to manage on your own. My intention with *e3 for LIFE* is to provide you with a lifestyle system that makes it easy for you to take back control over your health and happiness with ease. Having someone who you can share your successes with, as well as talk to in times of need, is crucial to ensure you stay the course to achieve *e3 for LIFE*. Support could come from a loving family member, a good friend, a personal trainer, or a coach. No matter where your support comes from, it is important to share your intentions with someone who will provide encouragement along the way.

Special Feature: Visit www.PowerofFood.com if you are ready for support as you strive to bring *e3 for LIFE* into your daily routine. I would be happy to be your source of support through my *Power of Food Nutrition Coaching* opportunities. You will begin experiencing results in a matter of days.

Along with following the *80/20 Rule* for FOOD, the 5 KEY STEPS should be followed daily. If you do, you will be sure to attain abundant health and happiness with ease.

I can't thank you enough for picking up *e3 for LIFE* and bringing it into your life. I would love to hear from you on your experience reading this book. I also encourage you to share it with a loved one if you found it valuable. I look forward to having you as part of the *Power of Food* community.

Your Friend in Health,

Adam Hart

To comment, please visit the following:
Website: www.PowerofFood.com/blog
Facebook: Power of Food or Adam Hart
Twitter: Power of Food
Email: info@poweroffood.com

e3 For LIFE RESOURCES

FOOD REFERENCES

"The Food Doctor" by Vicki Edgson and Ian Marber, Collins and Brown Ltd, 1999.

"The All in One Guide to Natural Remedies" by Dr. E. Ali, et al, Adi, Gaia, Esalen Publication Inc., 2001.

"Living the Good Life" by David Patchell-Evans, David Patchell-Evans, 2000.

"Earth Watch, Farmed Fish" by Paul Henderson, Vitality Magazine, October 2004.

"Wisdom of The Human Body: Part 1, The Digestive System" by Christine Crag, M.D., Kelowna B.C., email drcraig@Okanagon.net

"Fresh Produce Guide" by Dr. H. Richter M.D., Try-Foods International, Inc., 2003.

"The Vegetarian Way" by Virginia Messina, M.P.H., RD and Mark Messina, PhD, Crown Publishers, 1996.

"The Garden of Vegan" by Tanya Barnard and Sarah Kramer, Arsenal Pulp Press, 2002.

"How it All Vegan" by Tanya Barnard and Sarah Kramer, Arsenal Pulp Press, 1999.

"The Rock Warrior's Way" by Arno Ilgner, Desiderata Institute, 2003.

"Vegetarian Quick and Easy" by Troth Wells, New International Publications Ltd, 2000.

"Super Detox" by Michael van Straten, Quadrille Publishing Limited, 2003.

"Breathe Deeply" by Dr. Gordon Stewart, Vista magazine, Issue 36.

"Good Digestion" by Ken Babal, C.N., Alive Books, Vancouver, Canada, 2000. Alive Publishing Group, 1-800-663-6580. www.alivepublishing.com

"Principles of Anatomy and Physiology" by Gerard J. Tortora and SandraReynolds Grabowski. Biological Sciences Textbooks, 2003.

"The Road Less Traveled: Pursuing the Vegetarian Alternative" by Graham Bulter, C.N.P.A., Alive Magazine, August 2004.

"Healing Herbs" by Walter Kacera, D.N., Ph.D., A.H., New Direction Magazine, Oct/Nov 2004.

"The Complete Idiot's Guide to Total Nutrition" by Joy Bauer, M.S., R.D., C.D.N., Pearson Education, Inc., 2003.

"The Man's Health Book" by Michael Oppenheim, M.D., Prentice-Hall, Inc., 1994.

"Eat Smart, Think Smart" by Robert Haas, Think Tank International Corporation, 1994.

"Stretching" by Bob Anderson, Shelter Publications, Inc., 2000.

"Staying Healthy with Nutrition" by Elson M. Haas, M.D., Celestial Arts, 1992.

"Transforming Ourselves Transforming the World" by Brian K Murphy, Fernwood Publishing, 1999.

THOUGHTS & HABITS
REFERENCES

"A Diet for a New America" by John Robbins, H J Kramer and New World Library, 1987.

"Eating Alive, Prevention Thru Good Digestion" by Jonn Matsen, N.D., Crompton Books Ltd., 2002.

"The American Heritage® Dictionary of the English Language, Fourth Edition", Houghton Mifflin Company, 2004.

"The Columbia Electronic Encyclopedia, Sixth Edition", Columbia University Press, 2003.

"Fats and Oils" by U. Erasmus, Alive Books, 1986.

"The Thrive Diet" by Brendan Brazier, Penguin Group, 2007.

"The Healthy Kitchen" by Andrew Weil, M.D. and Rosie Daley, Alfred A. Knopf, New York, 2003.

"You. The Owner's Manual" by Michael F. Roizen, M.D., and Mehmet C. Oz, M.D., HarperResource, 2005.

"Allergies: Disease in Disguise" by Caroleen Bateson-Kotch, Alive Books, 1994.

"Hard to Swallow: The Truth About Food Additives" by Doris Sarjeant and Karen Evans, Alive Books, 1999.

"Spontaneous Healing" by Andrew Weil, M.D., Fawcett Columbine, 1995.

"The Food Connection" by Sam Graci, John Wiley and Sons, 2001.

"Prescription for Dietary Wellness" by Phyllis A Balch, Avery, 2003.

"The Intangibles of Leadership" by Richard A. Davis, Ph.D., Jossey-Bass, 2010.

"The Dream Manager" by Matthew Kelly, Hyperion, 2007.

"Law of Attraction" by Michael J. Losier, Michael J. Losier, 2006.

"The Power of Now" by Eckhart Tolle, Namaste Publishing, 1999.

"The Spontaneous Fulfillment of Desire" by Deepak Chopra, Three Rivers Press, 2003.

"Think and Grow Rich" by Napoleon Hill, Jeremy P. Thatcher/Penguin, 2005.

"A New Earth" by Eckhart Tolle, Plume, 2005.

"Cashflow Quadrant" by Robert Kiyosaki, Warner Business Books, 1999.

"The Secret" by Rhonda Byrne, Atria Books, 2006.

"Thresholds of the Mind" by Bill Harris, Centerpoint Press, 2007

"The 4-Hour Workweek" by Timothy Ferriss, Crown Publishers, 2007.

"The Power of Positive Thinking" by Norman Vincent Peale, Fawcett Crest, 1956.

"Secrets of the Millionaire Mind" by T. Harv Eker, HarperBusiness, 2005.

"Unlimited Power" by Anthony Robbins, Fawcett Columbine, 1986.

"Anatomy of the Spirit" by Caroline Myss, Ph.D., Three Rivers Press, 1996.

"The E Myth" by Michael E. Gerber,
HarperBusiness, 1995.

"Feel The Fear and Do it Anyway" by Susan
Jeffers, Ph.D., Fawcett Columbine, 1987.

"How to Win Friends and Influence People" by
Dale Carnegie, Pocket Books, 1936.

"Make Your Life a Masterpiece" by Peter Legge,
Eaglet Publishing, 2006.

"The Wealthy Barber" by David Chilton, Stoddart,
1989.

"The Intention Experiment" by Lynne McRaggart,
Free Press, 2007.

"In The Realm of Hungry Ghosts" by Gabor Mate,
M.D., Vintage Canada, 2008.

I invite you to visit
www.PowerofFood.com
for more amazing recipes,
videos and support through
my *Power of Food* Nutrition
Coaching Programs.

Adam Hart

LaVergne, TN USA
11 April 2011
223616LV00002B/2/P

9 781897 435458